HOUGHTON MIFFLIN HARCOURT

WRITE SOURCE

SkillsBook

GREAT
SOURCE.

HOUGHTON MIFFLIN HARCOURT

A Few Words About the
Write Source SkillsBook

Before you begin . . .

The *SkillsBook* provides you with opportunities to practice the editing and proofreading skills presented in the Student Edition. That book contains guidelines, examples, and models to help you complete your work in the *SkillsBook*.

Each *SkillsBook* activity includes a brief introduction to the topic and examples illustrating how to complete that activity. You will be directed to the page numbers in the text for additional information and examples. The "Proofreading Activities" focus on punctuation and the mechanics of writing. The "Sentence Activities" provide practice in sentence combining and in correcting common sentence problems. The "Parts of Speech Activities" highlight each of the eight parts of speech.

The Next Step

Most activities include a Next Step at the end of the exercise. The purpose of the Next Step is to provide ideas for follow-up work that will help you apply what you have learned to your own writing.

Photo Acknowledgments   Cover (flame) ©Alexey Stiop/Alamy; cover (tires) ©picturesbyrob/Alamy; cover (sunset) ©Corbis; cover (camera) Harcourt School Publishers; cover (video camera) ©Comstock/Getty Images; cover (headlights), cover (desert) ©Photodisc/Getty Images.

Trademarks and trade names are shown in this book strictly for illustrative purposes and are the property of their respective owners. The authors' references herein should not be regarded as affecting their validity.

Copyright © by Houghton Mifflin Harcourt Publishing Company

All rights reserved. No part of this work may be reproduced or transmitted in any form or by any means, electronic or mechanical, including photocopying or recording, or by any information storage or retrieval system, without the prior written permission of the copyright owner unless such copying is expressly permitted by federal copyright law.

Permission is hereby granted to individuals using the corresponding student's textbook or kit as the major vehicle for regular classroom instruction to photocopy entire pages from this publication in classroom quantities for instructional use and not for resale. Requests for information on other matters regarding duplication of this work should be addressed to Houghton Mifflin Harcourt Publishing Company, Attn: Paralegal, 9400 South Park Center Loop, Orlando, Florida 32819.

Printed in the U.S.A.

ISBN   978-0-547-48460-0 (student edition)

12 0928 18

4500705697   A B C D E F G

If you have received these materials as examination copies free of charge, Houghton Mifflin Harcourt Publishing Company retains title to the materials and they may not be resold. Resale of examination copies is strictly prohibited.

Possession of this publication in print format does not entitle users to convert this publication, or any portion of it, into electronic format.

Table of Contents

Proofreading Activities

© Houghton Mifflin Harcourt Publishing Company

Sentence and Paragraph Activities

© Houghton Mifflin Harcourt Publishing Company

Parts of Speech Activities

© Houghton Mifflin Harcourt Publishing Company

Prepositions

Conjunctions

Interjections

Parts of Speech

© Houghton Mifflin Harcourt Publishing Company

Proofreading Activities

The activities in this section include sentences that need to be checked for mechanics, spelling, or correct word choice. Most of the activities also include helpful *Write Source* references. In addition, the **Next Step** activities encourage follow-up practice of certain skills.

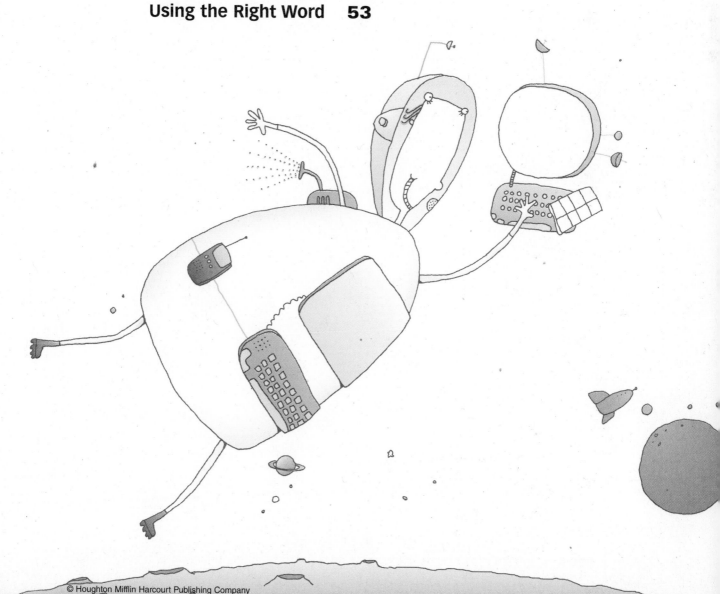

© Houghton Mifflin Harcourt Publishing Company

End Punctuation

Stop! Look? Listen. **End punctuation** is like a traffic cop. It controls the movement of your writing, telling the reader "Stop here!" It directs the reader to "ask a question," to "show emphasis," to "state a fact."

End punctuation marks—*periods, exclamation points, question marks*—make the reader put on his or her brakes at the end of each complete thought. (For more information about end punctuation and capitalization see 579.1, 580.1, and 580.4 in *Write Source*.)

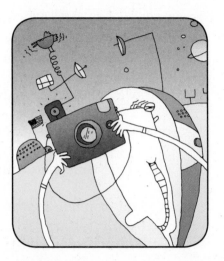

 **Directions**   Place periods, question marks, and exclamation points where they are needed in the following narrative. Also supply the necessary capital letters. The first paragraph has been done for you.

1   I had applied for a position on the yearbook staff during the first

2   week of school. what a thrill to find out I made it! was I going to be

3   able to do a good job? I would find out on group-picture day.

4   my friends and I were excited that it was finally group-picture

5   day Gabriella, Kim, and I were responsible for making sure that

6   everybody who was in a group got his or her picture taken what a

7   difficult job how could we be sure that everybody would be in the

8   right place at the right time were we up to this task we were about

9   to find out

10   we decided that the teachers themselves should make sure that all

11   of their activity members were at the right place at the right time for

12   the pictures we told the teachers to check off the students' names as

13   they arrived for their appointments we provided the checklists what

© Houghton Mifflin Harcourt Publishing Company

14   a great idea I'd like to take credit for the checklists unfortunately, I can't

15   it was Kim's brainstorm

16   we also made sure that announcements were made at regular

17   intervals so students were constantly reminded of the picture schedule

18   ahead of time one announcement read, "Please have students from

19   student council report to the multipurpose room " the announcements

20   were my responsibility

21   we scheduled all groups during the morning periods when no

22   students had gym would you want your picture taken in a "geeky"

23   gym suit what a fantastic system do it right, and it will go right

24   i'm happy that nothing went wrong as a matter of fact, everything

25   went very well the only thing the students had to do to get their

26   picture in the yearbook was listen for the announcements of their

27   activities and get checked off by their advisers of course, they also had

28   to smile and say, "cheeeeeese"

Next Step Write a journal entry about an experience in your life that first worried you but, when it arrived, turned out to be no problem at all. Organize your thoughts in chronological order and try to use transition words (*next, finally,* and so on). Don't forget to "spice up" your writing with the four different types of sentences: *commands, statements, exclamations,* and *questions.* When you are done, check your end punctuation.

© Houghton Mifflin Harcourt Publishing Company

Commas Between Items in a Series

Commas are needed to separate words, phrases, or clauses in a series. A series must always contain at least three items. (See 582.1 in *Write Source* for more information.) Items in a series should be parallel, or of the same type. A well-constructed series in which each item is of the same type will make your writing more balanced and will lead to smoother reading. In the sentence below, notice that *hit, run,* and *field* are all verbs in the same form. This makes them parallel.

Example

To Separate Items in a Series:
A good baseball player must be able to <u>hit</u>, <u>run</u>, and <u>field</u>.

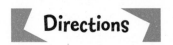 **Directions**   Insert commas where needed to separate items in a series in the sentences below. The first sentence has been done for you.

1. Hitting a ball, running the bases, and fielding a position demand different skills.

2. Most good hitters have great eyesight quick reflexes and strong wrists.

3. Knowing the pitcher's moves taking the longest possible lead and getting the jump on the catcher are essentials for a good base runner.

4. Fielding any position well requires having a strong throwing arm a knowledge of opposing hitters and an ability to move quickly in any direction.

5. Regular practice intense concentration and good coaching are all important factors in a player's development.

© Houghton Mifflin Harcourt Publishing Company

6. Enjoying the company of team members being out in the fresh air and getting some exercise are all benefits of playing baseball.

7. Do some warm-up exercises grab your glove and go play ball.

8. Individual sports like tennis golf and archery also have their rewards.

9. Golf can sometimes be a frustrating exasperating and challenging game.

10. Crooked drives erratic putts and topped balls can plague even the most enthusiastic golfer.

11. Sand traps water hazards and rough greens provide added difficulties.

12. Despite sliced drives lost balls and terrible scores, many enjoy nothing more than a good round of golf.

Next Step On your own paper, write five sentences. Use a parallel series of items in each sentence. Vary your series to include words, phrases, and clauses.

© Houghton Mifflin Harcourt Publishing Company

Commas to Set Off Nonrestrictive Phrases and Clauses

Commas are used to set off nonrestrictive clauses from the rest of a sentence. **Nonrestrictive clauses** are clauses that may be removed from a sentence without changing the basic meaning of the sentence. Study the examples below. (See 584.1 in *Write Source* for more about this use of commas.)

Examples

Nonrestrictive Clause:

Roger, who has passed all his finals, will graduate in June.

(The clause "who has passed all his finals" adds information to the sentence but is not necessary to make the basic meaning clear.)

Restrictive Clause:

Students who have passed all their finals will graduate in June.

(The clause "who have passed all their finals" is needed to make clear which students are eligible to graduate. It restricts the meaning of the sentence, so no commas are required.) **Note:** Phrases may also be restrictive.

 **Directions** Place commas around nonrestrictive clauses in the following sentences. (Do *not* place commas around restrictive clauses.) The first one has been done for you.

1. The American writer Ernest Hemingway was fond of Spain, which he visited many times.

2. Hemingway who traveled a great deal also spent time in France, Africa, and Cuba.

3. Hemingway's style which influenced thousands of writers appeared simple and effortless.

© Houghton Mifflin Harcourt Publishing Company

4. Hemingway who was a perfectionist would often write less than 500 words a day.

5. New York's Strand Bookstore which is the largest used-book store in the state contains more than eight miles of books.

6. Robert Frost who became America's best-known poet first gained fame in England.

7. The old book that Julie found was worth more than fifty dollars.

8. Soccer which has long been a favorite sport in Europe and South America is now becoming popular in the United States.

9. Babe Ruth who became baseball's greatest hitter began his career as a pitcher.

10. My little brother won't go back to the ballpark where he once got lost.

Directions Write three correctly punctuated sentences containing nonrestrictive clauses.

1. _____

_____

2. _____

_____

3. _____

_____

Next Step Exchange your sentences with a classmate. Check each other's sentences to see if they are correct. If there is any doubt about a particular sentence, see 584.1 in *Write Source* and make corrections.

© Houghton Mifflin Harcourt Publishing Company

Commas to Set Off Dialogue, Interruptions, and Interjections

In **dialogue,** commas are used to set off the exact words of the speaker from the rest of the sentence. Here is one example: "Don't mix dialogue and narrative," said the teacher, "but separate them with commas and quotation marks."

Brief shifts of focus in a sentence are also marked by commas. Shifting reflects natural breaks or pauses you might take when reading a passage aloud. Shifting might be caused by **interruptions, nouns of direct address,** or **interjections.** Notice the shifting in this sentence: "Yes, George, you did, as a matter of fact, receive the highest grade on the Mr. Wizard genius exam." (See the examples below and at 584.3, 588.1, 588.2, and 588.3 in *Write Source* for more information.)

Examples

The boss said, "You may have a raise."
(A comma sets off the speaker's exact words from the rest of the sentence.)

The raise, however, was small.
("However" is set off from the rest of the sentence because it interrupts the flow of the sentence and can be omitted without changing the basic meaning of the sentence.)

"Jack, did you know about the raise?" asked André.
(The person directly addressed—being spoken to—is set off with a comma.)

"Yes, I did."
(Interjections like "yes" and mild exclamations are separated from the remainder of the sentence by a comma.)

 **Directions** Place commas where needed in the sentences below. The first one has been done for you.

1.   "André, you know that assignment is due tomorrow," scolded Mary.

2.   André said "Why do you think I'm hurrying?" He as a matter of

© Houghton Mifflin Harcourt Publishing Company

3 fact didn't really seem to be in a big rush.

4 He had for example just used 20 minutes to type a single

5 paragraph.

6 "Gosh" Mary commented "if that's fast, I'd hate to see slow."

7 "Mary haven't you ever heard that haste makes waste?" asked André.

8 "Yes but I've also heard that late assignments get bad grades"

9 replied Mary.

10 "Mary I've never been late with an assignment yet, and I don't

11 intend to start now" André stated in his own defense.

12 "Well there's a first time for everything, so if I were you, I'd

13 hurry just a little" warned Mary.

14 "As a matter of fact I am thinking of ways to work faster" André

15 said slowly.

16 "Sure you are, Andre" said Mary.

17 "Say Mary I could work faster if I ate something" hinted André.

18 "Actually a snack is not a bad idea. I'll make some popcorn. You

19 start typing" replied Mary.

20 "Pizza sounds even better" André said, grinning, as his fingers

21 started to fly across the keyboard.

22 "Whoa I think we finally found the solution to your typing block"

23 laughed Mary.

Next Step Using your own paper, write two sentences for each of the four types of commas covered in this exercise. Read your sentences aloud to a classmate. Then trade papers and check each other's punctuation.

© Houghton Mifflin Harcourt Publishing Company

Commas to Separate Introductory Clauses and Phrases

A comma is used to separate an **introductory adverb clause** or a **long introductory phrase** from the independent clause that follows it. You should note, however, that no comma is required when a short introductory phrase begins the sentence or when the adverb clause follows the main clause. (Study the examples below and 590.1 in *Write Source* to help clarify these exceptions.)

Examples

In spring dairy farmers are busy planting crops.
(No comma is required after "spring" because the introductory phrase is short.)

After spring planting is done, there is still plenty to do.
(A comma sets off the introductory adverb clause.)

There is still plenty to do after spring planting is done.
(No comma is required because the adverb clause follows the main clause.)

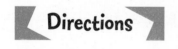 **Directions** Read the sentences below carefully, underline the main clauses, and insert commas where they are needed. There are three sentences that do not require commas. The first one has been done for you.

1. Regardless of the season or day of the week, dairy farmers have plenty to do to keep them busy.

2. Because cows do not observe holidays they must be milked every day.

3. If a farmer is to succeed he or she must follow nature's schedule.

4. With nature running the show the farmer has very little choice.

5. Modern equipment helps the farmer because it cuts out some of the backbreaking labor.

© Houghton Mifflin Harcourt Publishing Company

6. Over the next decade or two a farmer's day will probably get shorter as equipment increases his or her productivity.

7. Be it hail, wind, or drought farmers are at the mercy of the weather.

8. Rain is welcome during the summer although it can be a problem at harvest time.

9. In addition to late-season rains an early frost can also be damaging to a crop.

10. Although 12 hours is an average day farmers work longer during harvest.

11. Since harvesting is so important every working day is crucial.

12. As my neighbor John Williams once told me nature is the world's toughest boss.

13. John often complains about farming even though he loves his life on the farm.

14. For the past fifty years John has been a very good friend.

Next Step Take some time to review information on dependent and independent clauses in *Write Source*. Then, write your own paragraph about a favorite holiday that includes sentences with introductory phrases and clauses. When you are finished, check to make sure you have used commas correctly in your sentences..

© Houghton Mifflin Harcourt Publishing Company

Commas to Separate Equal Adjectives

Two or more adjectives that equally modify the same noun should be separated with commas. There are two simple "equality" tests. Try switching the order of the adjectives. If the meaning of the sentence remains clear, the adjectives are equal. You can also insert "and" between the adjectives. If the sentence makes sense and reads well, you can use a comma. Try both tests on the sentence below. (See 586.2 in *Write Source* for more information.)

Example

Decent, good-hearted people sometimes avoid homeless individuals.
(Both tests work for this sentence, so the adjectives are equal and require a comma.)

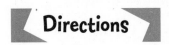 **Directions**   Insert commas between equal adjectives where needed. *Note:* Do not place a comma after the last adjective.

1. Healthy-looking well-dressed pedestrians often look away when they come in contact with ragged penniless street people.

2. What those fresh-scrubbed well-groomed people don't realize is that with a bit of bad luck they also might be begging on the corner.

3. Some of those unwashed undernourished homeless people may have held high-paying management jobs in the city.

4. Perhaps they owned spacious landscaped homes in the suburbs and drove sleek shiny cars.

5. Any confident successful person today could still face failure tomorrow.

6. Be careful before judging those who eat in soup kitchens and sleep on dangerous garbage-laden curbsides.

Next Step For each of the equal adjectives you found in the sentences above, substitute your own adjective.

© Houghton Mifflin Harcourt Publishing Company

Commas in Compound Sentences

A comma should be used with a coordinating conjunction between two independent clauses in a compound sentence. Coordinating conjunctions include these words: *but, or, nor, and, for, so,* and *yet.* Combining independent clauses to form compound sentences can add variety to your writing. (See 590.2 in *Write Source.*)

Example

Dalton eats too much, but he blames his weight on genetics.

(The comma and conjunction "but" are used to connect the two independent clauses in this compound sentence.)

Note: Do not confuse a simple sentence containing a compound verb with a compound sentence.

Dalton eats too much and blames his weight on genetics.

("Eats" and "blames" form the compound verb of a simple sentence.)

 **Directions** If the sentences below contain two independent clauses, add a comma before the conjunction. The first one has been done for you.

1. Dalton always smiles after losing a game, but he still hates losing.

2. Dalton thinks about how he played and practices for the next game.

3. It was too rainy to go in-line skating so we watched a video.

4. Jon wanted to shoot baskets with his dad but he had promised to go biking with his brother.

5. Lee usually loses at crossword games but always wants to play them.

6. She plays yet she never improves at crossword games.

7. Marcie bought a new dictionary and she plans to study it every day.

8. After school, Zeke e-mailed three friends and then delivered papers.

© Houghton Mifflin Harcourt Publishing Company

Comma Rules

The punctuation mark that has the most uses (and probably causes the most confusion) is the comma. You will want to become familiar with the comma rules. (See pages 582–590 in *Write Source*.)

 **Directions** Place commas correctly in each sample sentence. Then explain the rule that applies to that use of commas.

1. I love to spend time at amusement parks movies and concerts.

Rule: _____

_____

2. There were 4 0 0 0 0 people at the last concert I attended.

Rule: _____

_____

3. We ordered tickets from Ticketsellers 4004 West Main Street Chicago

Illinois 60010. The tickets will arrive by September 5 2010.

Rule: _____

_____

4. "Yes " said Dad "you can take some friends to the concert."

Rule: _____

_____

5. No we don't want to sit in the back rows of the stadium.

Rule: _____

_____

© Houghton Mifflin Harcourt Publishing Company

6. The front row if you asked me would be the best place to sit.

Rule: _____

_____

7. We were going to take the van but it wouldn't start.

Rule: _____

_____

8. Tickets came addressed to Leroy Adams D.D.S. and Peter Kendall Ph.D.

Rule: _____

_____

9. We beamed with joy as we held the expensive long-awaited tickets.

Rule: _____

_____

10. After many months passed the day of the concert arrived. During that seemingly endless wait another act had been added to the show.

Rule: _____

_____

11. Outdoor concerts aren't my favorite but they are fun in good weather.

Rule: _____

_____

12. My dad an expert concertgoer was a big help in our planning.

Rule: _____

_____

© Houghton Mifflin Harcourt Publishing Company

Commas with Appositives

An appositive is a word or phrase that identifies or renames a noun or pronoun. Here's a chance for you to practice using commas to set off appositives. Review the examples below before you begin your work. (See 586.1 in *Write Source* for more examples.)

Examples

Oahu, an island in Hawaii, is a favorite vacation spot.
A favorite vacation spot is Oahu, an island in Hawaii.
(Commas are used to set off the nonrestrictive appositive "an island in Hawaii" because the appositive phrase is not needed to understand the basic meaning of the sentence.)

The popular vacation spot Oahu is one of the Hawaiian Islands.
("Oahu" is a restrictive appositive identifying "popular vacation spot." Commas are not used to set off a restrictive appositive because it is needed to understand the basic meaning of the sentence.)

> **Directions** Underline the appositives in the sentences below. Add commas where necessary. The first two have been done for you.

1. My only sister, Jennie, has a hamster and two goldfish.

2. Her goldfish Stella chases the other one around the tank.

3. The other fish Sid tries to hide in the plants.

4. Jennie thinks she might have to buy another goldfish a new friend for Stella and Sid.

5. My two brothers Bill and Sam do not have any pets.

6. My brother Bill had fish when he was younger.

7. Bill says that maybe Jennie the only animal lover in our family should trade the hamster for a new goldfish.

8. He suggested that Jennie name the new fish Marlon.

© Houghton Mifflin Harcourt Publishing Company

Comma Review

Here's a chance to practice two more uses of commas. Review the examples below before you begin your work. (Also see 584.1 in *Write Source* for more examples.)

Examples

A comma is used to set off a nonrestrictive clause:

The report, <u>which was thoroughly researched</u>, received an A+.

(The clause "which was thoroughly researched" is purely descriptive and could be eliminated without changing the meaning of the sentence. Commas are required.)

A comma is not used to set off a restrictive clause:

The law <u>that the Senate passed last week</u> requires us to obey the curfew.

(The clause "that the Senate passed last week" is necessary to the meaning of the sentence.) ***Note:*** When you are trying to decide whether to start your clause with *which* or with *that,* use *which* for nonrestrictive clauses and *that* for restrictive.

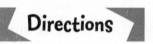 **Directions** Underline the restrictive clauses and the nonrestrictive clauses in the sentences below. Add commas where necessary.

1. My cousin's bus is one of the new ones that run on natural gas.

2. My bus which is one of the old yellow ones runs on smelly diesel fuel.

3. When my driver is late which is unusual she says it's because she doesn't have enough passengers.

4. Traffic is a problem because there are too many people who are driving their own cars instead of taking buses.

5. Alex who has a chronic cough says that air pollution is a bad problem in our city.

6. There would be less traffic and less pollution if more people who now ride alone in their cars rode buses.

7. Alex's method of getting to school which is walking doesn't pollute.

© Houghton Mifflin Harcourt Publishing Company

Semicolons

A semicolon sometimes acts like a period and sometimes acts like a comma. (For information about semicolons, see page 594 in *Write Source*.)

Examples

To Join Two Independent Clauses:
I have a signed Batman comic; it is the most valuable book I own.

To Join Two Independent Clauses Connected by a Conjunctive Adverb:
My karate instructor was tough; however, he never got upset.
(Conjunctive adverbs include *also, as a result, besides, for example, furthermore, however, in addition, instead, meanwhile, moreover, nevertheless, similarly, then, therefore, thus.*)

To Separate Groups of Words or Phrases That Already Contain Commas:
My favorite foods are pizza with pepperoni, peppers, and mushrooms; peanut butter and jelly sandwiches; and liver and onions.

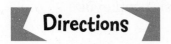 **Directions** Place semicolons where appropriate in the following sentences. The first sentence has been done for you.

1. John decided to go to a moviehe wanted to see *Deep Impact*.

2. Afterward, he said he didn't care for the film he said he is getting tired of "disaster" movies.

3. Victor likes most films nevertheless, he still refuses to see *Titanic*.

4. He won't go to war movies he classifies them as "disaster" films.

5. Victor thinks there are enough real disasters around he doesn't need them magnified on a wide screen with Dolby surround-sound.

6. Victor may be right however, I was impressed by *Titanic* and loved being scared by *Deep Impact*.

© Houghton Mifflin Harcourt Publishing Company

7. I enjoy all kinds of movies therefore, I don't plan to change my movie-going habits.

8. My cousin T. J. likes fantasies, comedies, and thrillers, doesn't like romances, and refuses to see horror films.

9. I hate to get to the movies late I want to see the previews.

10. I don't like to eat when I'm watching movies besides, the food at the theater is so expensive.

11. People at the theater are sometimes rude it can make the whole experience unpleasant.

12. Some people talk during the feature, get up to get food, go to the bathroom, or just change seats and once someone fell asleep behind me and started snoring.

13. New theaters with stadium-style seating are nice most people like them.

14. I really like discount theaters you can get a ticket and a big tub of popcorn for the same price as a ticket at a regular theater.

15. Sometimes I go to the discount theater even if I could rent the same movie at a video store it's just more fun watching a movie on a big screen.

Next Step Now it's your turn to try the three different uses for the semicolon. Write a sentence of your own for each semicolon use covered in this exercise.

© Houghton Mifflin Harcourt Publishing Company

Colons

A colon may be used to introduce a list or an important point. A colon can also set off a word or phrase from the rest of the sentence for emphasis. A colon follows the salutation of a business letter and comes between numbers that show time. (See page 596 in *Write Source* for additional information about colons.)

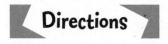

Examples

Dear Mr. Valenza:
(The colon follows the salutation of a business letter.)

Musician Wanda Landowska made this statement: "I never practice; I always play."
(The colon is used to formally introduce the quotation.)

Most burglaries take place between 1:00 a.m. and 4:00 a.m.
(The colon is used between numbers showing time.)

A good student does the following: reads, writes, and remembers.
(The colon introduces a list.)

The police were missing one important piece of information: a motive.
(The colon sets off the phrase "a motive" for emphasis.)

> **Directions** Place colons where they are needed in the following sentences. The first two sentences have been done for you.

1. There was one problem with the 7:00 a.m. class: the time of day.

2. Dad's sports rules were the following: play hard, play fair, and play often.

3. John gave us some good advice for losing weight eat less.

4. He also told us to avoid the following eating between meals, eating before going to bed, and eating foods that are mostly sugar or salt.

© Houghton Mifflin Harcourt Publishing Company

5. The library doors were locked at exactly 500 p.m.

6. Lucas has three major dislikes whiners, bullies, and braggarts.

7. On the other hand, there was one thing he really liked football.

8. Some follow this saying "Children should be seen and not heard."

> **Directions** ▸ Rewrite the sentences below so that each sentence uses one or more colons. The first sentence has been done for you.

1. Reading, sleeping, and eating are Aaron's favorite activities.

Aaron's favorite activities are the following: reading, sleeping, and eating.

2. Chad was lost in the woods from ten in the morning until eleven at night.

_____

_____

3. He dropped his backpack and spilled energy bars, a water bottle, and his flashlight.

_____

_____

4. "It's always darkest before dawn" was my grandfather's favorite saying.

_____

_____

5. The one thing I liked about Uncle Bill was listening to his scary campfire stories.

_____

_____

Next Step Write a paragraph that includes at least three of the different uses of colons.

© Houghton Mifflin Harcourt Publishing Company

Punctuating Dialogue

Having a conversation is simple. Someone says something. Someone else responds, and a conversation is under way. Written conversations are a little more difficult. They need to be correctly punctuated to make sense. (Study the examples below; then see 598.1, 598.2, and 600.1 in *Write Source* for help.)

Examples

"I'm tired," said Mark. "This broken arm is wearing me out."
(A period comes after "Mark" because that's the end of a complete sentence.)

"Oh yeah," joked Ken, "you need to give your arm a rest."
(A comma comes after "Ken" because what follows completes the sentence.)

"Is that the best broken-arm joke you can think of?" Mark asked.
(The question mark is placed inside the quotation marks because the quotation is the question.)

Directions ▸ Punctuate the following sentences with quotation marks, commas, and end marks. The first one has been done for you. (*Note:* See how correct punctuation makes the dialogue easier to follow.)

1   "Jessie, I think you dropped your pen," warned Jon. Jessie started

2   searching for her pen.

3   Have you done the English homework asked Jessie It's really long

4   No replied Jon I haven't read it yet I planned to read it in the

5   library this afternoon.

6   Don't forget said Jessie you also have to write an essay.

7   It's a good thing you reminded me because I had forgotten all

8   about the essay Jon said.

© Houghton Mifflin Harcourt Publishing Company

9   I'll be thinking about you slaving away while I'm enjoying the

10   movie gloated Jessie

11   What are you going to see asked Jon

12   I'm going to rent *Titanic* Jessie responded

13   Yeah the special effects in *Titanic* are awesome Jon said I'm

14   really not into disaster films that much

15   I'm not usually either said Jessie but I have a special interest in

16   this one My great-grandparents were supposed to have been on that

17   ship

18   Wow Jon said That's a case where missing the boat was a good

19   thing

20   Well I just hope you don't miss the boat with that English

21   assignment Jessie said as she went out the door

Next Step Here's your chance to get a little creative with dialogue. Make up a dialogue between two fictional persons. Don't explain who the characters are or what the situation is about. Rather, let the characters develop naturally during the conversation. Continue the dialogue until you come to a natural stopping point. Make sure to punctuate your sentences correctly.

© Houghton Mifflin Harcourt Publishing Company

Quotation Marks and Italics

When you've written a story or an essay that contains a book title or a slang word or the title of a favorite TV show, you must decide whether to **italicize** that piece of information or put **quotation marks** around it. Titles of longer works—and the names of ships and aircraft—should be italicized. Articles, book chapters, and television episodes are enclosed in quotation marks.

Also, a word or phrase being used in a special way, or a word that is slang, is enclosed in quotation marks. (See 600.2–600.3 and 602.3 in *Write Source*.)

 **Directions** Underline titles that should be in italics and insert quotation marks where needed. The first one has been done for you.

1. Because of television spin-offs and films, the starship <u>Enterprise's</u> "continuing mission" seems destined to go on forever.

2. He's such a good player, the others say he's bad.

3. Air Force One is the name of a plane and the title of a film.

4. I think Stopping by Woods on a Snowy Evening is one of Robert Frost's best poems.

5. My father's least favorite word is bugged.

6. My mother reads the New York Times, Newsweek, and the Washington Post to keep up with current news.

7. My favorite song from Paul Simon's Graceland album is You Can Call Me Al.

© Houghton Mifflin Harcourt Publishing Company

Directions In the following paragraph, properly punctuate titles, names of spacecraft, words used in a special way, and slang expressions.

1   Why are movies like Star Wars so successful? What was the appeal of

2 sending astronauts on the Apollo missions to the moon? Because much of

3 Earth has been explored, space and aliens have become the new frontier. The

4 introduction for the TV series Star Trek always included the words to boldly

5 go where no man has gone before. People want to know what space is really

6 like and whether people on Earth are all alone in the universe. Discover,

7 Scientific American, and the Smithsonian are just a few magazines that

8 include articles about the exploration of space. The television show X-Files

9 was based on the idea that other intelligent life not only exists, but also is

10 here on Earth. An old movie like 2001: A Space Odyssey argues that human

11 life has aliens to thank for human progress. So, NASA continues to send

12 spacecraft to discover what is out there. The Mars rover Spirit moves across

13 the Martian landscape looking for secrets to unlock about that nearby planet.

14 In the magazine Nature, the article Voyager Reaches the Final Frontier

15 explains that the Voyager 2 space probe has left our solar system and some

16 day may reach other worlds. Some people think all this is a waste of money,

17 but others say this is cool. A poem called Songs and a musical piece entitled

18 Rocketman show how much the exploration of space has taken hold of our

19 imaginations. People are drawn to the unknown, the Final Frontier.

Next Step Think of several titles of movies and magazine articles. Now write a sentence or two using those titles. Be sure to punctuate the titles correctly.

© Houghton Mifflin Harcourt Publishing Company

Apostrophes 1

The possessive of singular nouns is usually formed by adding an apostrophe and an *s*, as in the examples below. (See 604.4 in *Write Source* for more information.)

Examples

To Form Singular Possessives:

Mr. Brown's assignment

(For most nouns, add an apostrophe and an "s.")

the Rio Lobos's depth *(or)* **the Rio Lobos' depth**

(For singular, multisyllable nouns ending with an "s" or a "z" sound, add an apostrophe and an "s" or an apostrophe only.)

the moss's color

(For one-syllable nouns ending in "s," add an apostrophe and an "s.")

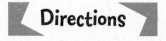 **Directions** Write the correct singular possessive form above each underlined noun in the following sentences. The first sentence has been done for you.

John's
1. Did <u>John</u> team win the soccer tournament?

2. The <u>girl</u> dress was too formal for the party.

3. It was <u>somebody else</u> loss, not mine.

4. The <u>boss</u> salary was much larger than mine.

5. My <u>sister-in-law</u> car was a bright red convertible.

6. They found the <u>student</u> book in the back of the classroom.

7. <u>Massachusetts</u> population is large compared to its small size.

8. The messy room was my <u>brother</u>.

9. Your guess is as good as <u>Ms. Jenks</u> guess.

10. The mountain <u>pass</u> elevation was 10,500 feet.

© Houghton Mifflin Harcourt Publishing Company

Directions Write the correct possessive form above each underlined singular noun in the following sentences. The first one has been done for you.

1. That *dress's* dress buttons are carved from ivory.

2. Someone else opinion may be different from mine.

3. My brother-in-law opinion sometimes differs from mine.

4. In fact, his opinion seems different from almost everyone.

5. Jane team won the championship.

6. St. Louis main tourist attraction is the Gateway Arch.

7. What is jazz fascination?

8. Anyone ticket will get you into the concert on the green.

9. What wit said, "Yesterday news is good for wrapping fish"?

10. Tess final-exam grade was higher than mine.

11. Did Texas population increase by more than a million in the last decade?

12. The room appearance could best be described as chaotic.

13. Bill always gives a day work for a day pay.

14. Bob and Matt's boats are tied at the dock.

15. John always appreciates his mother-in-law humor.

Next Step On your own paper, write the possessive form for each of the words listed below.

1. somebody
2. gas
3. anyone
4. Dallas
5. Max
6. month
7. everyone
8. father-in-law

© Houghton Mifflin Harcourt Publishing Company

Apostrophes 2

An apostrophe is used to show that letters have been left out of words (don't), to show possession (Garfield's dinner), and to indicate time or amount (a day's work, a dollar's worth). (Read the example below; then see 604.1, 604.4, and 606.5 in *Write Source* for more information about apostrophes before you complete the following sentences.)

Example

"Didn't your sister's puppy chew up yesterday's homework, Homer?"
(In the word "didn't" the apostrophe shows that the letter "o" has been left out; in "sister's" the apostrophe shows possession for the singular noun "sister"; in "yesterday's" the apostrophe indicates time.)

 **Directions** — Add apostrophes to the following sentences. The first sentence has been done for you.

1. "I'll get to tomorrow's assignments after this TV show," I called.

2. Moms answer was, "No you wont. Youll work on them right now."

3. Mr. Basss homework wasnt too hard. It was the algebra I couldnt face.

4. Besides that, when the seasons new shows were on, it was hard to do work.

5. "Cant I take a break, Mom?" I pleaded as though my brains well-being was

   at stake.

6. "Youve been on break!" was my moms reply.

7. I shouldve finished my homework in study hall, but instead I helped Mr.

   Anderson with his bulletin board entitled "The Class of '05 in the Workplace."

© Houghton Mifflin Harcourt Publishing Company

8. Im learning that when students homework isnt done, it comes back to haunt

them, so I started to work.

9. Whats going to be first, math problems or history?

10. What Id thought would be an hours worth of math, I completed in 15

minutes.

11. Historys next, I thought, and started without a moments delay.

12. Reading about wars makes a person appreciate soldiers sacrifices.

13. Soon I forgot Id been overloaded with three teachers assignments.

14. The evenings fears of bad grades in my classes vanished in the next 30

minutes, and the next days homework was completed.

15. My advice: Get tomorrows homework done today, or itll become

tomorrows nightmare!

Next Step Review the rules for possessives in the "Proofreader's Guide" in *Write Source* and then add apostrophes as needed in the following phrases:

❑ Fuddle, Muddle, and Bamboozles magic act

❑ Leonardos, Raphaels, and Michelangelos pizzas

❑ my brother-in-laws yo-yo

❑ their sisters-in-laws roller skates

❑ everybodys pet rock

❑ yesterdays fads

© Houghton Mifflin Harcourt Publishing Company

Apostrophes 3

The plural possessive of nouns ending in *s* is usually formed by adding an apostrophe after the *s*. Plural nouns not ending in *s* usually require an apostrophe and an *s*. (See 606.1–606.3 in *Write Source* for rules governing shared possession and the possessive of a compound noun.)

 **Directions**   In the space provided, write the possessive form of each plural noun below. The first one has been done for you.

_____*women's*_____   **1.** The <u>women</u> order for concert tickets was made in person.

_____   **2.** The boys, girls, and <u>parents</u> applause shook the rafters.

_____   **3.** The <u>bosses</u> rules were strict.

_____   **4.** The <u>brothers-in-laws</u> cars were identical.

_____   **5.** The <u>toys</u> storage box was broken.

_____   **6.** The <u>Joneses</u> family tree went back to the Civil War.

_____   **7.** Two <u>months</u> worth of mail had collected on the porch.

_____   **8.** The <u>girls</u> opinions were extremely divided.

_____   **9.** The <u>boys</u> teams all won their games.

_____   **10.** Who designed the <u>mens</u> uniforms?

_____   **11.** The <u>bosses</u> offices are upstairs.

_____   **12.** The <u>players</u> meals will be served in the gym.

© Houghton Mifflin Harcourt Publishing Company

Directions In the space provided, write the correct plural possessive form of the nouns listed. Add a word or two to complete the phrase. The first one has been done for you.

1. the girl   *the girls' project* _____

2. the dog _____

3. the child _____

4. the boss _____

5. the man _____

6. the team _____

7. the herd _____

8. the ex-president _____

9. the pilgrim _____

10. the boy _____

Directions On the lines below, write three sentences containing plural possessives. Use a noun ending in "s," a noun not ending in "s," and a plural compound noun. (An example of a plural compound noun is "brothers-in-law.") Do not use nouns listed in this exercise.

1. _____

_____

2. _____

_____

3. _____

_____

© Houghton Mifflin Harcourt Publishing Company

Hyphens 1

Hyphens are used to divide words at the end of a line. They are also used between numbers in fractions, to join certain letters and words, and to avoid awkward spellings. (See 608.4, 610.2, and 610.3 in *Write Source* for more about using hyphens.)

Examples

She won the race by six-tenths **of a second.**
(The hyphen is used between numbers in the fraction.)

I bought my T-shirt **at the concert.**
(The hyphen joins a letter and a word.)

She had to re-create **her report after her soda spilled on it.**
(The hyphen avoids confusion in the word "re-create.")

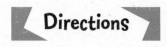 **Directions** Divide the following words as they should be divided at the end of a line. If the example is already divided correctly, write "C" in the space; if the example is incorrect, write out the word and hyphenate it correctly. The first two have been done for you.

1. cau-ght _____*caught*_____
2. es-cape _____*C*_____
3. hea-ven _____
4. does-n't _____
5. e-rased _____
6. hyp-hen _____
7. div-ide _____
8. fract-ion _____
9. re-fer _____

10. bro-ken _____
11. par-agraph _____
12. taught _____
13. sud-den _____
14. num-ber _____
15. cent-er _____
16. tour-ist _____
17. can-dy _____
18. his-to-ry _____

© Houghton Mifflin Harcourt Publishing Company

34

Directions Place hyphens as needed in the following sentences. The first sentence has been done for you.

1. Yesterday my cousin turned twenty-one.

2. He moved the high jump bar exactly one quarter of an inch higher for a record setting attempt.

3. My parents wouldn't let me see the R rated movie.

4. The game was three fourths over, and Bob hadn't missed a single three point shot.

5. He came back from Chicago with a fashionably ragged pair of jeans and his usual start of winter cold.

6. We will have to recover the chair because it looks too worn to go with our new indoor outdoor carpeting.

7. The standard photos come only in four inch widths; enlargements come in 5 by 8 inch or 9 by 12 inch sizes.

8. The Kennedy Nixon television debate is an important event in political history.

9. His self conscious cousin was nervous about performing in the third grade holiday pageant.

10. We need to recruit six 12 year old girls for our volleyball team.

Next Step Create new words beginning with the prefixes *self, all,* and *great*. Write a sentence for each word.

© Houghton Mifflin Harcourt Publishing Company

Hyphens 2

Hyphens may be used to form compound words, new words using certain prefixes and suffixes, and single-thought adjectives. (See 608.2, 608.3, and 610.1 in *Write Source* for additional examples of the uses of hyphens.)

Examples

I hit fast-forward **to watch my favorite part of a movie.**
("Fast-forward" is a compound word.)

***The Wild Bunch* is my** all-time **favorite western.**
("All-time" is a new word formed by combining the prefix "all" with "time.")

My collection of award-winning **films includes 20 comedies.**
("Award-winning" is a single-thought adjective modifying "films.")

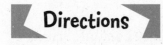 **Directions** Read the sentences below and insert hyphens where necessary between compound words, single-thought adjectives, and new words formed by using prefixes and suffixes. The first one has been done for you.

1. People probably should eat more fat‿free foods.

2. Hard to understand instructions seem like they are written in Greek.

3. The heart pounding ending left me breathless.

4. The "easy to follow" instructions for the new DVR confused me.

5. The new book of student written poems was high on my must read list.

6. The 12 year old skating champion fell after trying the triple jump.

7. I stopped at a fast food deli for lunch.

8. The one run loss was becoming routine for the hard luck baseball team.

9. I want to replace an ink jet printer with an up to date laser model.

10. The company halted in house production of its magazine.

© Houghton Mifflin Harcourt Publishing Company

Dashes

You probably will not find many reasons to use dashes in your writing. Still, you should know when and how to use dashes. (Review the examples below and see 612.1–612.3 in *Write Source* for additional explanations and examples.) You should note that in any typed work, dashes are formed by two hyphens (--), without spacing before or after.

Examples

The 1998 New York Yankees were an amazing team—in fact, an astonishing team—during regular and postseason play.
(To indicate sudden breaks in sentences.)

After winning the American League championship, the team had a final goal—sweeping the World Series.
(To set off a word, a phrase, or a clause for emphasis.)

Oh no—not that—yes, I heard you, but I can't believe it.
(To show interrupted speech.)

Directions In the sentences below, insert dashes where they are needed. The first one has been done for you.

1. The 1998 Yankees had one aim and one aim only 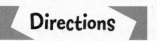∧winning.

2. I think the Yankees proved proved beyond a shadow of a doubt that they had more overall talent than anyone else.

3. After 162 regular season games and 15 postseason games, the players had one thing in mind a long vacation without any baseball.

4. Playing more than 170 games can be wearing even on the most dedicated player.

5. Each Yankee player received something special a World Series ring.

Next Step Using the sentences above as models, write your own five sentences about a favorite sports team. Include each of the three uses for a dash at least once. Read your sentences aloud to a classmate.

© Houghton Mifflin Harcourt Publishing Company

Other Forms of Punctuation

As the thoughts you express in writing become more complex, punctuation marks become more important. Some of the most useful punctuation marks are *brackets [ ]*, *ellipses [. . .]*, and *parentheses [( )]*. (See pages 612 and 614 in *Write Source* for information about these special forms of punctuation.)

 **Directions** Using the information in *Write Source*, explain the rule that applies to the punctuation mark used in each sentence below. The first one has been done for you.

1. "Can I . . . um . . . borrow your baseball glove . . . please? I can't find mine . . . and practice starts in twenty minutes," Marco pleaded.

Rule: **An ellipsis is used to show a pause in dialogue.**

_____

2. My grandmother joined the Peace Corps after hearing Kennedy say, "Now the trumpet summons us again . . . to bear the burden of a long twilight struggle . . . against the common enemies of man: tyranny, poverty, disease, and war itself. . . . Will you join in that historic effort?"

Rule: _____

_____

3. "[Ronald Reagan] was the oldest person to be elected president."

Rule: _____

_____

4. The pizza order forms (for the school fundraiser) were handed in to the teacher.

Rule: _____

_____

© Houghton Mifflin Harcourt Publishing Company

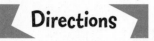

Directions

On the lines provided, copy the paragraph below. Omit the words that are underlined and replace the boldfaced pronoun. Use the correct punctuation to show the changes you made. Also add parentheses where necessary.

Dr. Martin Cooper may not be a familiar name, but he invented one of the most significant innovations of the twentieth century: the cell phone. Dr. Cooper, an electrical engineer, created the first portable handset. Then, in April of 1973, he made the first cell phone call. He was standing on a street outside his Manhattan hotel when he made the call to a base station on the roof of the Burlington Consolidated Tower now the Alliance Capital Building in New York. Could **he** have imagined that day, as passersby stared at him, that 35 years later nearly everyone would have a cell phone?

_____

_____

_____

_____

_____

_____

_____

_____

© Houghton Mifflin Harcourt Publishing Company

Punctuation Review

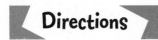 **Directions** Read the paragraphs below carefully. Draw a line through any errors in punctuation and capitalization. Add punctuation and capitalization as needed. The first few errors have been corrected for you.

1   "The Murders in the Rue Morgue," a short story by Edgar Allan

2   Poe, is thought to be the first example of the detective story. Although

3   Poe's character C. Auguste Dupin may have been the first fictional

4   detective he is by no means the best-known that honor certainly

5   falls to Sir Arthur Conan Doyle's immortal Sherlock Holmes Holmes

6   who is known to millions of readers and viewers around the world

7   first appeared in 1887. Doyle's books as well as numerous films and

8   television shows feature Sherlock and his constant companion,

9   Dr. Watson

10   The reasons for Holmes enduring popularity are themselves a

11   bit of a mystery for in many ways Holmes was not a very likeable

12   person. He was short tempered and he was unkind to other detectives,

13   especially Police Inspector Lestrade of Scotland Yard.

14   Holmes's ever questioning mind and dislike for displays of emotion

15   made him appear cold calculating and uncaring. He was an expert

16   violin player and could play beautifully when he felt like it Holmes

17   in fact was very moody. When he had nothing to occupy his mind he

18   became bored and depressed. He would sit around for days making

© Houghton Mifflin Harcourt Publishing Company

19 horrible squawks and screeches on the violin, which drove Dr. Watson

20 nearly crazy.

21   holmes was not exactly a picture perfect roommate either. He left

22 chemicals for his scientific experiments all over the place and he kept

23 his smelly messy pipe tobacco in his old, bedroom slippers. He stuck

24 his mail to the mantle with a penknife and he stashed his many

25 book's and papers wherever it seemed convenient at the time.

26   Despite Holmes cool personality and his weird personal habits

27 Watson was genuinely fond of him and although he rarely showed it

28 Holmes also cared deeply for his friend. When Doyle made it appear

29 that Holmes had died while fighting with Dr. Moriarty Holme's

30 toughest opponent the reaction against Doyle was tremendous. People

31 responded as though a longtime personal friend had died real people

32 seemed just as upset as the fictional Dr. Watson at the report of

33 Holmes death. After three years Watson and thousands of fans

34 breathed a sigh of relief when Sir Arthur Conan Doyle brought Holmes

35 back.

Next Step Once you go through this exercise finding as many errors as you can, you might want to check your answers with a classmate (if your teacher doesn't object). If you discover differences in your corrections, you might want to discuss them and check in *Write Source*. Then make additional corrections as needed.

© Houghton Mifflin Harcourt Publishing Company

Capitalization 1

For most people, capitalizing the first word in a sentence is pretty automatic. It is knowing when to capitalize all the other words that is the greater challenge. (Add to your capitalization know-how by becoming familiar with pages 618–626 in *Write Source* and then try the exercises that follow.)

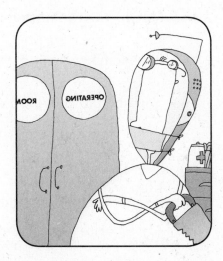

Directions   Underline the word or words that need capitalization in each sentence below. Then write each capitalized word or words in the space above the error. The first one has been done for you.

Mayor William James

1. After the win, <u>mayor william james</u> arranged for a victory parade.

2. I went out and joined uncle bill, who was sitting on the porch steps.

3. Brody's interest in martial arts came from his study of asian culture.

4. My sister wrote a long paper for her american literature course.

5. I would not want to have lived in the middle ages.

6. The operation will be performed by dr. karl jacobs.

7. My brother found it hard to adjust to the slower pace of the south.

8. I plan to read the short book *flowers for algernon* this weekend.

9. Juan is helping me learn to speak and read spanish.

10. I don't know where our family is going for easter vacation.

11. My mother added to her collection of african art on her last trip to Kenya.

12. How will the green bay packers do this year?

13. Eric didn't realize he was part of an fbi investigation.

© Houghton Mifflin Harcourt Publishing Company

14. When was the united nations formed?

15. The democratic party was proud to have him as a member.

16. You should take interstate 95 all the way into the city.

17. Did you know you have to take a year of latin to graduate from some

    high schools?

18. My favorite part of the trip to Georgia was the southern cooking.

19. How does the west coast compare to where you lived before?

20. I heard the dave matthews band was recording a new album.

21. After the game, everyone went to the new pizza restaurant on

    midway boulevard.

22. Climbing to the top of the washington monument is one of my goals.

> **Directions**
>
> In the sentences below, put a line through any unnecessary capital letters and write the correct small letter above the line. The first sentence has been done for you.

1. The large truck turned *e*/East at the edge of town.

2. My Mom and Dad met Aunt Thelma at the Hospital.

3. Next Tuesday will be the first day of Spring.

4. Lucas hadn't counted on failing his Math test.

5. Wheatums Cereal is my favorite breakfast food.

6. To find the Stadium, turn South on North Avenue.

7. The High School is located on Jackson Street.

© Houghton Mifflin Harcourt Publishing Company

Capitalization 2

Here's another exercise to help you capitalize words correctly. (See pages 618–626 in *Write Source* for more information on capitalization.)

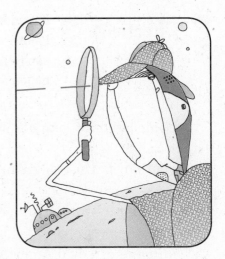

Directions ▷ Each sentence below has at least one error in capitalization. There may be more than one error in some of the sentences. Underline each error and write the correction in the space above the line. The first sentence has been done for you.

        dad   *FBI*   *New York City*

1. Chen's <u>Dad</u> worked for the <u>fbi</u> in the <u>new york city</u> office.

2. He investigated the world trade center bombing.

3. The FBI often works with Local Police Agencies such as the new york city police department.

4. Crimes such as Terrorism and Kidnapping come under FBI jurisdiction.

5. the FBI's advanced crime-fighting facilities are used by local Police Departments.

6. The bureau keeps a Fingerprint File containing millions of fingerprints.

7. Chen's dad talked to our History class when we studied Law Enforcement.

8. He was a Trial Lawyer before becoming an FBI Agent.

9. He also told us stories about j. edgar hoover's fight against Organized Crime.

10. Today the FBI works with nasa, the irs, and other Government Organizations.

© Houghton Mifflin Harcourt Publishing Company

Directions For additional practice, find the errors in capitalization in the sentences below. There may be more than one error in each sentence. Underline each error and write the correction in the space above the line. (See pages 618–626 in *Write Source* for help.)

1. Someone once jokingly said that anyone who doesn't like Professional Football is Un-American.

2. Judging from the way people react each year to the super bowl, there are millions of Loyal Americans.

3. All of the eighth graders from central middle school are going to the football hall of fame in canton, ohio, during their class trip this Spring.

4. My friend Danny is a native american, and he is very anxious to see what the hall of fame contains about Jim Thorpe and other old-time players.

5. danny just finished reading a book called *The Early Years Of the NFL*.

6. My friend billy is from the south, and he wants to see all the quarterbacks from southern colleges that are in the hall of fame.

7. His current favorite player is brett favre, the quarterback who went to college in mississippi and now plays for the green bay packers.

8. Billy says that a lot of Quarterbacks from Southern colleges are actually from the north.

Next Step Write a paragraph about the town or city you live in. Include where your town is located and some of places you like the most. Check your use of capitalization and then read your paragraph aloud to a classmate.

© Houghton Mifflin Harcourt Publishing Company

Capitalization and Abbreviations

Attention to detail means different things depending on the task, but the result will always be the same: a better party, a tastier pizza, and a finer piece of writing.

In this activity you will review a series of phrases or sentences to make sure that capital letters and abbreviations have properly been put in place. (See pages 618–626 in *Write Source* for more information on capitalization and abbreviations.)

 **Directions**
Put a line through any word or letter below that is capitalized, lowercased, or abbreviated incorrectly. Correct each error. One way to do this would be to go through the list once and make the changes you're sure of. Then, for those that you question, review the rules in *Write Source*. The first sentence has been done for you. (*Note:* Do not abbreviate the names of states, countries, months, days, or units of measure in formal writing. Also do not use signs or symbols [%, &] in place of words.)

1. We are looking for a project for our ~~s~~pringfield ~~m~~iddle ~~s~~chool ~~g~~lobal ~~s~~tudies
   ~~F~~   *January*
   ~~f~~air held in ~~jan.~~

2. How about a fiesta highlighting mexican culture?

3. what a great idea for the middle of Winter!

4. mr. brown, our Social Studies teacher, is asking each class to do its part.

5. our class, global studies 101, will bring the food.

6. mister brown says that other classes will be responsible for planning the

   schedule of events by this Wed.

7. Should we get parents involved from the springfield parent teacher assoc.?

© Houghton Mifflin Harcourt Publishing Company

8. Yes, we need a lot of help and maybe a few $'s, too.

9. The fiesta will involve spanish music and festival customs from Mex.

10. mr. whitman, the gym teacher, will teach all of the Eighth Graders the

    mexican hat dance.

11. in the Art Classes, all of the students will make posters and wall decorations.

12. The springfield middle school band will perform special music for the fiesta.

13. the band director, mr. ames, has written an original fiesta song, and he tells

    us it's called "the old brown dog."

14. We can't wait to hear the song, which he wrote for jazz, his french poodle.

15. He's a very creative person, and he sings like sting.

16. The chorus 102 class will sing back-up with miss thompson.

17. we're calling the event springfield's fiesta fantastic.

18. The South end of the Gym is reserved for the Piñata bashing.

19. Springfield's fiesta Fantastic is scheduled for jan 30.

20. the *Springfield daily Trib.* will come and take pictures.

21. what a great way to study the spanish-mexican cultures!

Next Step Remember or imagine a time when you and a teacher worked together on a project. It could have involved something fun like planning an assembly program or an end-of-the-year cleanup, or something as serious as organizing a tornado or fire drill. Write a paragraph or two about this experience. Exchange finished products with a partner and check carefully for capitalization and abbreviation errors.

© Houghton Mifflin Harcourt Publishing Company

Abbreviations and Numbers

Some abbreviations may be used in formal writing (*Ms., Mr., Mrs.*); others may not (*yr.* for *year*). (See examples below and pages 618–626 in *Write Source* for additional information on abbreviations and when to use them. Then see pages 634–636 for basic rules covering the use of numbers.)

Examples

Abbreviation: **Mr.** (Mister)

Acronym: **CARE** (Cooperative for American Relief Everywhere)

Initialism: **CIA** (Central Intelligence Agency)

Decade: **1880s** (*not* eighteen eighties)

Specific Year: **1952** (*not* nineteen fifty-two)

 **Directions** Correct the errors in the use of abbreviations and numbers in the sentences below. Underline each error and write the correct form in the space above the error. The first sentence has been done for you.

    FBI   *United States*

1. The <u>f.b.i.</u> has jurisdiction over federal crimes within the <u>U.S.</u>

2. During the nineteen thirties, bank robbers stole thousands of $'s, and many

  of the robbers ended up on the bureau's "Most Wanted" list.

3. FBI agents caught 2 of the country's most famous bank robbers, John

  Dillinger & Baby Face Nelson.

4. After J. Edgar Hoover took charge in nineteen twenty-four, the FBI became

  more effective in fighting crime.

5. Mr. Hoover prosecuted 100's of criminals each yr.

© Houghton Mifflin Harcourt Publishing Company

6. 6 members of our school newspaper collaborated to write 2 5-pg. articles

based on interviews with former FBI agents.

7. They learned that approx. sixty agents out of every 100 had received

training as either lawyers or accountants before joining the FBI.

 **Directions** Opposite each number below, list the matching common term or its abbreviation. Some of the answers may come from your general knowledge. (Some of the answers may be found on page 634 in *Write Source*.) The first one has been done for you.

Term	Abbreviation
1. ante meridiem	*a.m. or A.M.*
2.	HWY or hwy.
3.	NY or N.Y.
4. Doctor	
5. compact disc	
6.	WWW
7. Boulevard	
8.	Mr.
9. Alaska	
10. post meridiem	

Next Step Write five original sentences using numbers. Exchange your sentences with a classmate and edit each other's sentences for usage errors. If you find errors, discuss the corrections and review rules in *Write Source*.

© Houghton Mifflin Harcourt Publishing Company

Mechanics Review

Directions > Read the paragraphs below carefully. Correct spelling and capital letters where necessary and also make corrections where needed in the use of plurals, abbreviations, and numbers. Underline any error and write the correction in the space above the error. The first one has been done for you. (See pages 618–651 in *Write Source*.)

Last

1   <u>last</u> year my family moved from a small town in Northern ohio to New

2   York city. In the beginning, I was amazed at how different the states are—

3   Ohio from New York—and how different the midwest is from the east, but I

4   was really amazed at the difference between life in small-town america and

5   life in the big City. A number of surprises came when I started attending

6   High School in sept.

7   The 1st surprise was the size of the school. The building seemed to take

8   up an entire city block. The 2nd surprise involved class sizes. 20

9   students was an average-sized class in William Howard Taft high, my old

10   school; forty students was an average-sized class here at central high.

11   In addition to the sheer number of students, the number of different

12   nationalities was incredible. I felt as if I had wandered into a meeting of the

13   united nations. I met students from columbia, India, and china my first day in

14   school, & I discovered they were only a small % of the more than fifty

15   different nationalities represented at this High School. While I was walking

16   through the halls, I could hear a dozen different languages.

17   At lunch that first day, I met Harjot Singh, who came from India. I

© Houghton Mifflin Harcourt Publishing Company

18 found out that Harjot lived in my nieghborhood. he was nice enough to

19 invite me to his house to sample indian cooking.

20   It was a good thing Harjot offered his help after school on that first

21 day, too. If he hadn't, I might still be trying to figure out which Subway to

22 take to get home. Astonished by how crowded it was at the station, I was

23 frozen in confusion as carloads of passengers left the station. The map of

24 subway routes provided by the transit authority was meaningless to me. It

25 looked more like a diagram of the veins and arterys in the human body than

26 a map of train rts.

27   Even when Harjot pointed out the right train, I almost missed it

28 because I was listening to 3 musicians playing banjoes. A poke in the ribs

29 from Harjot reminded me to pay more attention. A subway platform is no

30 place to be daydreaming.

31   I found Harjot's advice and information about getting along in the city

32 useful from the very begining. Now that I have spent a full yr. in new york

33 at my new school, I have come to realize how helpful he was to me in

34 100 and one different ways. I also am gratful to Harjot's Mom for all that

35 great indian food.

Next Step Using your own paper, describe a time when you were in an unfamiliar
situation and someone offered you assistance that really helped you out. Then, exchange
papers with a friend and read his or her story carefully, underlining any errors. Once
you get your story back, make any necessary corrections to your own work.

© Houghton Mifflin Harcourt Publishing Company

Plurals and Spelling 1

Making the plural form of most nouns is easy. All you do is add *s* to the singular. But there are always exceptions. (See pages 630–632 in *Write Source* for more information.)

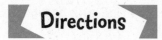 **Directions** After each singular word below, write the plural form of the word. The first one has been done for you.

1. cup   *cups*
2. roof
3. mile
4. sister-in-law
5. mouthful
6. child
7. deer
8. hoof
9. cry
10. thief
11. loaf
12. solo
13. box
14. pen
15. pailful

16. monkey
17. knife
18. life
19. key
20. goose
21. radio
22. donkey
23. fox
24. dress
25. piano
26. marker
27. chief
28. tomato
29. lunch
30. dish

© Houghton Mifflin Harcourt Publishing Company

Plurals and Spelling 2

There are a number of rules for forming and spelling plurals correctly. There are also some general spelling rules to help you as you write. (See page 642 in *Write Source* for this information.)

Directions In the space next to each misspelled word below, write the correct spelling. Write "C" if the spelling is correct. The first one has been done for you.

1. admitance _____admittance_____   9. useful _____

2. prefered _____   10. acheive _____

3. ladys _____   11. trys _____

4. happyness _____   12. trying _____

5. monkies _____   13. niether _____

6. weird _____   14. foriegn _____

7. neice _____   15. huming _____

8. useing _____   16. begining _____

Note: There are some exceptions to most of the spelling rules. Keep a list of these words, or try to memorize them. Also, review the hints for becoming a better speller in *Write Source*.

Next Step Keep your own list of challenging words based on the spelling list in *Write Source* and your reading. Follow the steps to becoming a better speller until you master the first list. (Start with 10 words.) Have a classmate test your mastery of your words. Make a habit of adding and mastering new words each week. Be certain you know the meaning as well as the spelling for each word on your list.

© Houghton Mifflin Harcourt Publishing Company

Using the Right Word 1

It's important to use the right word whenever you share your thoughts in writing. You'll find definitions of the following words and more examples on pages 652–660 of *Write Source*.

Examples

The yacht has a sleeping berth below.
Royal subjects celebrated the prince's birth.

The kids didn't understand Mr. Allen's allusion to Bozo the Clown.
The wolf I thought I saw must have been an illusion.

The town's annual Labor Day parade was canceled.
Many stores hold biannual, or semiannual, sales every January and July.
We didn't meet last year, so our biennial family reunion will be held this year.

The rock climber carefully made her ascent up the face of the cliff.
Unfortunately, Mom and Dad were in complete assent regarding my punishment.

Annick carries her books in a canvas bag.
Candidates canvass the city before elections.

Some trees bear fruit in the fall.
Winter's bare trees can be dramatic.

I got a detention for my coarse language.
Keiji took a foreign language course.

Show me how to play that chord.
Use strong cord on that package.

Directions Draw a line through any incorrect underlined word and write the correct form above it. Do not change a word that is correct. The first sentence has been done for you.

1. A mama <u>bear</u> who has recently given ~~<u>berth</u>~~ *birth* is very protective of her cubs.

2. After making an <u>allusion</u> to *trompe l'oeil* in my art <u>coarse</u>, the teacher <u>canvassed</u> the students to see who knew its meaning.

3. Trompe l'oeil, which is French for "trick the eye," is a style of painting that creates an <u>allusion</u> of three-dimensional space.

© Houghton Mifflin Harcourt Publishing Company

4. While some trompe l'oeil artists paint on <u>bear</u> walls, others use <u>canvass</u>.

5. Every other year as a child, Aunt Gertrude's family took their <u>biannual</u> train trip.

6. As the train struggled to make its <u>assent</u> up steep hills, she slept comfortably in her <u>birth</u>.

7. A <u>chord</u> made of <u>course</u> twine held the puppet stage curtains open.

8. Every March and September, Karin plays a <u>cord</u> or two on her guitar to mark the beginning of our <u>semiannual</u> meeting.

9. Will the committee <u>ascent</u> to our amazing plans for this year's <u>annual</u> fund-raiser?

10. I can't <u>bare</u> the suspense.

Next Step Write a sentence for each of the following pairs or sets of words: *accept, except; already, all ready; capital, capitol; fewer, less; principal, principle;* and *who, whom.* (Use one set of words per sentence.) Then check your word usage by looking up each word in *Write Source.* Make any necessary changes.

© Houghton Mifflin Harcourt Publishing Company

Using the Right Word 2

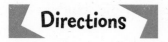

The following examples will help you determine if the words are used correctly in the exercise below. (Also see pages 662–668 in *Write Source*.)

Examples

Their personalities complement **each other.**
Everyone enjoys receiving compliments.

There are continual **announcements.** **Lottery winners need financial** counsel.
The speaker makes a continuous **buzz.** **Ms. Carmel serves on the city** council.

Her flair **with the flute was well known.** **Carefully** lay **the lamp on its side.**
A fire will flare **up in windy conditions.** **The tots will** lie **down for their naps now.**

As Juan pointed to his teeth, Maggie asked, "What are you trying to imply?**"**
"Shall I infer **from your actions that I have something stuck in my teeth?"**

> **Directions** If the underlined word is incorrect, cross out the word and write the correct form above it.

1. Raheem and Tavon are <u>continuously</u> repairing their skateboards.

2. They asked Zane for <u>council</u> about adding some <u>flair</u> to their boards.

3. Zane suggested that a dragon would nicely <u>compliment</u> Tavon's board.

4. "Fire <u>flairing</u> from its nostrils," he said, "would <u>infer</u> fierceness."

5. Raheem is sure he'll get <u>complements</u> if he can finish his board with some super-shiny varnish.

6. The National Safety <u>Counsel</u> advises boarders to always wear safety gear.

7. Tavon <u>inferred</u> that the organization was suggesting <u>continuous</u> wear, so he wears a helmet and padding even when he <u>lays</u> down to sleep for the night!

© Houghton Mifflin Harcourt Publishing Company

Using the Right Word 3

The following examples will help you determine if the words are used correctly in the exercise below. (Also see pages 670–674 in *Write Source*.)

Examples

The pain of loss is real.
The door needs a new pane of glass.

Like my mom, I don't care for liver.
As Dad drives, I read him stories.

The main bus stops at the train.
Shoshone brushed the horse's mane.

My belt buckle is metal.
The Olympic athlete won a gold medal.

"It's your moral duty to be good," Grandma says.
Six losses left the team with low morale.

The browned peaks of meringue on the pie pique my appetite.
The neighbor peeks at us from behind her curtain.

Directions Draw a line through any incorrect underlined word and write the correct form above it. Do not change a word that is correct.

1. Chad drew mountain <u>peeks</u> in the condensation on the <u>pain</u> of his window.

2. Coach Grayson had not told Chad that his injury might cost the team a chance for a <u>metal</u> at the tournament.

3. Chad's limp must have <u>peaked</u> Grayson's curiosity.

4. <u>As</u> Chad thought it over, he <u>piqued</u> at himself in the mirror.

5. His hair, which looked <u>as</u> a lion's mane, hadn't been washed in days.

6. His knee <u>pane</u> had lowered his <u>moral</u> more than he thought it would.

7. The basketball team's <u>mane</u> playoff game was Saturday.

8. Would he need a <u>medal</u> brace to play this weekend?

© Houghton Mifflin Harcourt Publishing Company

Using the Right Word 4

Many words that writers often find confusing are called **homophones.** Homophones are words that sound alike but are spelled differently. *To, two,* and *too* are homophones. (See pages 678–686 in *Write Source* for information about commonly misused words. Some of those words will be homophones.)

Examples

Xiang is smarter than I am.
It was then that we discovered the bones.

The wet dog shook water all over us.
Campers can whet their tools with rocks.

I think this is your calculator.
You're coming to my party, aren't you?

She's a little vain about her looks.
There's a W on the weather vane.
A nurse took blood from a vein in my arm.

Minnie has a sore wrist.
Jacinda wants to soar like an eagle.

The weather here can vary quite a bit.
Anita is a very talented writer.

Whose computer crashed?
Please see who's at the door.

Thomas Jefferson was the president who called for exploring the West in 1803.
The trip, which took more than two years, became famous.
Lewis and Clark led that expedition.

That woman, who is an alto, is also the choir director.
Aunt Jackie, whom I admire, earned a college scholarship.

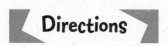 **Directions** Circle the correct word in each set of words. The first sentence has been done for you.

1   It was later (*than*, *then*) I thought it was. I made my way to Dani's

2   house, (*who, which, that*) was halfway up a (*vary, very*) steep hill. The wind

3   whipped the windsock, and the post of the weather (*vain, vane, vein*) was

4   bending in its fury. It wasn't raining yet, but if I didn't hustle, I'd be all (*wet,*

5   *whet*) by the time I got there.

© Houghton Mifflin Harcourt Publishing Company

6   "(*Your, You're*) late," Dani said as she opened the door.

7   "I'm sorry. I can't walk as fast because my ankle is still a bit (*soar,*

8   *sore*)," I said.

9   Dani's mom, (*whose, who's*) smooth black hair fell almost to her waist,

10   said hi. She is a beautiful woman, but she is not (*vain, vane, vein*) about it.

11   She said she would show me how to (*vary, very*) my hairstyle sometime. "We

12   can try some braids in (*your, you're*) hair," she said.

13   (*Than, Then*) Dani pulled me down the hall. "Guess (*whose, who's*)

14   coaching the team this summer," she said so excitedly that a (*vain, vane,*

15   *vein*) in her forehead bulged. I made a few incorrect guesses and said,

16   "Okay, you've (*wet, whet*) my interest. (*Who, Whom*) is it?"

17   "Do you remember the guy (*who, which, that*) coached Amy's team last

18   summer?" she asked.

19   "Sure," I said. "Amy's team won the championship."

20   "He's going to coach our team," Dani said. "This year, it'll be our team

21   (*who, which, that*) (*soars, sores*) to the top!"

22   We did a little dance for the coach with (*who, whom*) we would surely

23   have a winning season.

Next Step Try writing a tongue twister using homophones that begin with the letter "b." (See *Write Source* for help.)

© Houghton Mifflin Harcourt Publishing Company

Using the Right Word Review 1

Directions 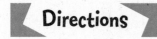 Draw a line through any incorrect underlined word and write the correct form above it. Do not change a word that is correct. The first line has been done for you. (See pages 652–686 in *Write Source* for information on using the right word.)

1   Last year, Carlos worked with the Watsonville fireworks team, ~~that~~ *which* put

2   together the Fourth of July fireworks display. He was able to do so because

3   his uncle owns the company, Fire in the Sky, Inc. Uncle Diaz, <u>whom</u> works

4   with medium-sized communities, likes Watsonville. He enjoys this town

5   because the town <u>counsel</u> wants something special, realizes its funds are

6   limited, but finds donations to provide an exciting celebration.

7   Last year was special for Carlos not only because he worked with his

8   uncle but also because an extra-special rocket was fired <u>like</u> a grand finale.

9   It was billed as much louder and having greater special effects <u>then</u> any of

10   the other fireworks. During the months of May and June, Carlos would stop

11   by to check on the great rocket. Carlos wasn't allowed to work in the factory,

12   but he was able to visit. He <u>piqued</u> at every project on the tables. He was

13   <u>as</u> a reporter, constantly asking questions. His uncle would laugh and say,

14   "Your questions are like a string of firecrackers."

15   Finally, the big day arrived. Carlos was under no <u>allusions</u>; he knew

16   he could not be on the firing line. However, his uncle let him walk through

© Houghton Mifflin Harcourt Publishing Company

17 the <u>mane</u> area where the display was set up. Uncle Diaz carefully explained

18 how the system worked; his crew used an electrical-firing control panel. He

19 told Carlos that the <u>ascent</u> of the big rocket would be more rapid and more

20 dramatic than any of the other shots. The work Carlos had to do was hard,

21 but he didn't complain. After finishing his job, he collapsed on a spot of

22 <u>bear</u> ground totally worn out.

23   A little bit later, Uncle Diaz surprised Carlos by telling him that he

24 would fire the last rocket, the big rocket. Wow! What a <u>moral</u> booster. Carlos

25 was so excited he scarcely noticed the <u>continuous</u> firing of the other rockets

26 during the regular performance. <u>Than</u>, the moment came. Uncle Diaz,

27 <u>that</u> handed Carlos the control, told him to push the button. The rocket

28 seemed to sit still forever, but all of a sudden it roared into the sky, its fiery

29 <u>coarse</u> climbing higher and higher. Finally, the great rocket exploded with

30 a tremendous boom, filling the sky with long, streaming <u>flairs</u> of light. It

31 seemed like the birth of a star. The explosion was so loud, Carlos thought

32 every <u>pain</u> of glass in town must have broken. People loved it. Carlos could

33 hear them cheer, clap, and honk their car horns. It was a successful ending

34 to a fine fireworks performance. Uncle Diaz told him to <u>lie</u> the remote

35 control on the table and help break down the site. He ran to take the <u>canvas</u>

36 off the back of the truck. He felt good about the <u>complement</u> his uncle had

37 given him. He wants to help his uncle again this summer.

© Houghton Mifflin Harcourt Publishing Company

Using the Right Word Review 2

 **Directions** In the following sentences, draw a line through any incorrectly used word and then write the correct usage above it. Read each sentence carefully before making any corrections. (See pages 652–686 in *Write Source* for information on using the right word.)

1. It's difficult to peak through this windowpane because it's textured.

2. I cannot bare to lay around, but my doctor says, "Rest your sore ankle."

3. When I twisted it, I felt more pain then I'd ever felt before.

4. Your supposed to pull the chord for this light to come on.

5. If people tell you that you run as a gazelle, you may safely infer that they admire you're grace.

6. Nori showed her courage as she fearlessly reached the peek of the mountain.

7. The continuous hum which comes from the refrigerator keeps Sunila, whom is a vary light sleeper, awake at night.

8. Don't lie your towel too near the water, or it will get wet.

9. Whose going to canvass the teachers on this issue?

10. The school holds its annual parent-teacher conferences at the end of the first and third quarters.

11. Fiona, who's mom is an artist, gets canvass at a discount for our art class.

© Houghton Mifflin Harcourt Publishing Company

12. My music teacher, who I really like, complements my piano playing.

13. She says that I have a flare for playing classical music and has

counseled me to continue in that vain.

14. In her music appreciation coarse, we are currently studying the birth

of the blues.

15. Rock music's main influence was the blues, that made some people

question its morale value.

16. Nevertheless, the music of the first rock artists would wet the public's

appetite for more rock, and its assent in popularity was no allusion.

© Houghton Mifflin Harcourt Publishing Company

Sentence and Paragraph Activities

The activities in this section cover three important areas: (1) the basic parts of sentences and paragraphs, (2) common sentence errors, and (3) ways to add variety to sentences. Most activities include a main practice part in which you review, combine, or analyze different sentences. In addition, the **Next Step** activities give you follow-up practice with certain skills.

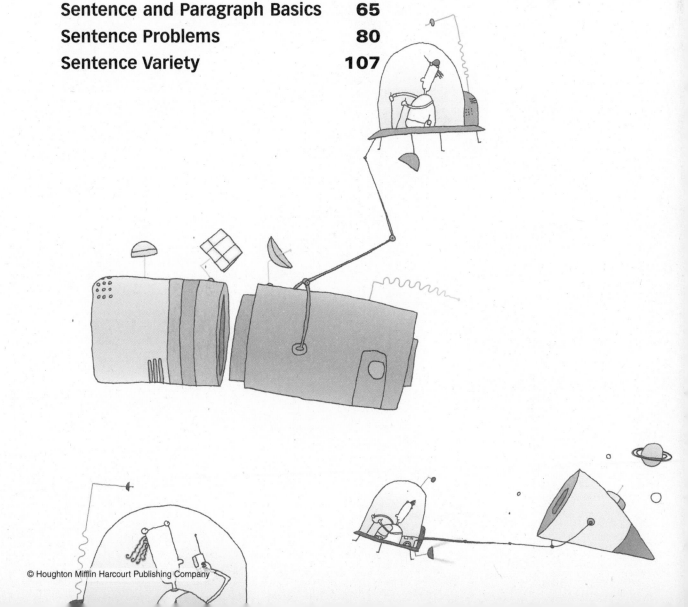

© Houghton Mifflin Harcourt Publishing Company

Subjects and Predicates

A sentence consists of two parts: a subject and a predicate. The **subject** is the part of the sentence that is doing something or about which something is said. The **predicate** (or verb) is the part of the sentence that says something about the subject. Each sentence has a *simple subject* and a *complete subject* and a *simple predicate* and a *complete predicate*. (For more information, see pages 501–502 in *Write Source*.)

Example

The very idea of computers terrified my dad completely.

("Idea" is the simple subject of the sentence. "The very idea of computers" is the complete subject. "Terrified" is the simple predicate. "Terrified my dad completely" is the complete predicate.)

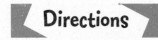 **Directions** In each of the following sentences, place parentheses around the simple subject and draw a line under the complete subject. Draw a circle around the simple predicate and draw a double line under the complete predicate. (*Note:* A simple subject or predicate may also serve as the complete subject or predicate.) The first sentence has been done for you.

1. My younger (sister) (convinced) Grandpa to get a computer.

2. Grandpa stared at the box the computer arrived in without touching it.

3. He looked at the box as if expecting it to explode.

4. I assembled the components under Grandpa's suspicious gaze.

5. Our brand-new monitor blinked to life.

6. My grandpa's mistrust of the computer lessened over the next few weeks.

7. He loves to send e-mails to his family and friends now.

© Houghton Mifflin Harcourt Publishing Company

Directions In each of the following sentences, place parentheses around the simple subject and draw a line under the complete subject. Draw a circle around the simple predicate and draw a double line under the complete predicate. The first sentence has been done for you.

1. Violent (thunderstorms) (hit) my hometown during the summer.

2. The first few storms had been typical summer rains.

3. The storms became more intense by late June.

4. Storm warnings were given almost daily throughout the month of July.

5. It was hard to plan ahead.

6. An uneasy feeling was settling in throughout the town.

7. The feeling grew stronger every day.

8. People began acting in unusual ways.

9. Bob jumped nervously at every sudden sound.

10. Showing how upset he was, Dan snapped at his little brother.

11. Mary heard strange noises around her house after dark.

12. Everyone was hearing strange things.

13. Things started to return to normal by early August.

14. It was a summer to remember.

Next Step Write three sentences describing either a rainstorm or a snowstorm. Then in each sentence (1) put parentheses around your simple subject, (2) draw a line under the complete subject, (3) draw a circle around your simple predicate, and (4) draw a double line under the complete predicate. Now read your simple sentences without any of the modifiers. Have you met the sentence requirement? Is there a subject (noun or pronoun) and predicate (verb) in each sentence?

© Houghton Mifflin Harcourt Publishing Company

Compound Subjects and Predicates

A sentence that contains two or more simple subjects has a **compound subject.** A sentence that contains two or more simple predicates has a **compound predicate.** A sentence may have a compound subject, a compound predicate, or both. (See page 501 and 690.4 and 692.6 in *Write Source* for more information.)

Note: Do not confuse a simple sentence containing compound subjects or compound predicates with a compound sentence. A compound sentence contains *two simple sentences* joined by a comma with a coordinating conjunction or joined by a semicolon. A compound sentence has a subject and a verb in each independent clause.

Examples

Compound Subject:
Carlos and Andre love pasta.

Compound Predicate:
Carlos eats fettuccine and devours tortellini.

Compound Sentence:
I like pasta, but meatballs make me ill.

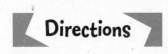 **Directions** In the following sentences, underline the simple or compound subjects with one line and the simple or compound predicates with two lines. In the blank before each sentence, label a simple sentence "S" and a compound sentence "C." The first sentence has been done for you.

_____C_____ **1.** Sheri and Aretha spoke at the meeting, and Mary took notes.

_____ **2.** I fell asleep and missed the meeting.

_____ **3.** You can watch television or finish your homework.

_____ **4.** Bill and Jim bought a new board and played darts for hours.

_____ **5.** Billy played hard but lost the game anyway.

© Houghton Mifflin Harcourt Publishing Company

_____ 6. The ship sank, but the crew launched the lifeboats and escaped.

_____ 7. Carlos, Juan, and Nancy were finalists in the poster contest.

_____ 8. I liked Juan's poster, but the judges awarded the prize to Carlos.

_____ 9. Bacon and eggs is a standard American breakfast.

_____ 10. The green and white car skidded and swerved down the street.

_____ 11. John, Bill, and Juan joined the Fox River Chess Club and played every Thursday afternoon.

_____ 12. The Dale twins looked alike, and they often dressed alike, too.

_____ 13. The boy with red hair delivered newspapers up and down the street.

_____ 14. Would you please open the window and air the smoke out of this room?

_____ 15. The lake shimmers a thousand gleaming lights by day, but it is dark and still at night.

_____ 16. The weary group of hikers trudged up the hill and down the valley.

Next Step Write five sentences describing a hike or trip you took. Make sure each sentence has a compound subject or compound verb (or both). Then in each sentence, underline the simple or compound subjects with one line and the simple or compound predicates with two lines.

© Houghton Mifflin Harcourt Publishing Company

Phrases and Clauses 1

Phrases and clauses are like a series of building blocks in the process of making sentences. **Phrases** are related groups of words lacking a subject or predicate (or both). Phrases can serve the same purposes as single words. Then there are clauses. **Clauses** are related groups of words that have a subject and a predicate. (See page 517. Also see 698.1–698.3 and 700.1–700.2 in *Write Source* for more information.)

Examples

Phrases:

the startling new book = noun phrase (It has no predicate.)

had been written = verb phrase (It has no subject.)

in six months = prepositional phrase (It has no subject or predicate.)

Independent Clause:

The startling new book had been written in six months.

An *independent clause* has a subject and a predicate. It can stand as a sentence because it contains a complete thought and makes sense.

Dependent Clause:

Since the startling new book had been written in six months . . .

A *dependent clause* has a subject and predicate, but it cannot stand as a sentence because it depends on another part of the sentence to form a complete thought.

 **Directions** Label each group of words below as a phrase or clause. Write "P" in front of the group of words if it is a phrase; write "IC" for an independent clause or write "DC" for a dependent clause. The first one has been done for you.

_____P_____ **1.** ran down the hill

_____ **2.** the man with the big smile

_____ **3.** when he saw the results of the race

_____ **4.** after the rain had stopped

_____ **5.** having been thoroughly soaked

© Houghton Mifflin Harcourt Publishing Company

_____ **6.** I finally bought a raincoat

_____ **7.** which was supposed to be guaranteed weatherproof

_____ **8.** standing on the corner

_____ **9.** waiting for the bus

_____ **10.** patiently with 50 other people

Directions ▷ Choose five of the phrases or dependent clauses from the exercise above. Then use them to create five independent clauses that can stand as individual sentences in the spaces provided below. (*Note:* You can combine the exercise material or add your own words to make your sentences.)

1. _____

_____

2. _____

_____

3. _____

_____

4. _____

_____

5. _____

_____

Next Step Try writing the wackiest sentence you can based on the material in the exercise. (Combine the exercise material, if you like, or add your own words to make your sentence.) Share your sentences with the class. See who wrote the funniest sentence.

© Houghton Mifflin Harcourt Publishing Company

Phrases and Clauses 2

Sentences are composed of phrases and clauses. A phrase is a group of related words that lacks either a subject or a predicate (or both). (See pages 516–517 in *Write Source* to review phrases and clauses. Also see 698.1–698.3 and 700.1–700.2.)

Examples

Phrases:

crossed the street
(The phrase does not have a subject.)

the small boy in the green coat
(The phrase does not have a predicate.)

about five feet away
(The phrase does not have a subject or a predicate.)

Independent Clause:

The small <u>boy</u> in the green coat <u>crossed</u> the street.

An *independent clause* has a subject and a predicate. It can stand as a sentence because it contains a complete thought and makes sense.

Dependent Clause:

When the small <u>boy</u> in the green coat <u>crossed</u> the street . . .

A *dependent clause* has a subject and predicate, but it cannot stand as a sentence because it depends on another part of the sentence to form a complete thought.

 **Directions** In the blank in front of each group of words below, label each phrase with a "P." Label each independent clause with "IC" and each dependent clause with "DC." The first one has been done for you.

___DC___ **1.** When my grandma went to elementary school

_____ **2.** Country school with only two rooms for grades 1 through 6

_____ **3.** Thirty students in the entire school

_____ **4.** Grades 1 through 3 were in one room

_____ **5.** Grades 4 through 6 in the other

© Houghton Mifflin Harcourt Publishing Company

_____ **6.** The schoolrooms were heated by wood-burning stoves

_____ **7.** Two teachers arrived early each morning to start the stoves

_____ **8.** Before students arrived

_____ **9.** Classes started at 8:00 a.m. and ended at 4:00 p.m.

_____ **10.** Fifteen-minute recess in the middle of the morning

_____ **11.** Played games in the school yard

_____ **12.** Because swings and seesaws are popular among younger students

_____ **13.** Some older students helped teachers

_____ **14.** Younger students with their lessons

_____ **15.** Coming in from recess, they were cold

_____ **16.** After they warmed their hands by the stove

_____ **17.** They had to write spelling words on a slate

_____ **18.** Tried not to waste paper

_____ **19.** Math was done on the slate, too

_____ **20.** Grandma home for lunch

_____ **21.** Older students learned to use a quill pen

_____ **22.** School was hard but a lot of fun, according to Grandma

Next Step How would you like to attend a two-room country schoolhouse like the one outlined in the exercise above? Write a paragraph describing why you would or wouldn't want to attend such a school. You might also want to talk to your grandparents, or some other people who are older, to find out what it was like when they went to school. Be sure all your sentences are complete and include some complex sentences (ones with both dependent and independent clauses).

© Houghton Mifflin Harcourt Publishing Company

Phrases and Clauses 3

An **adverb phrase** is a group of related words, lacking either a subject or predicate (or both), that modifies a verb, an adjective, or another adverb. An **adverb clause** is a dependent clause that modifies a verb, an adjective, or another adverb. Adverb clauses are formed using subordinating conjunctions. (See 700.2, 744, and 746.1 in *Write Source* to review subordinating conjunctions and adverb clauses.)

Examples

I slept so soundly last night. **(adverb phrase)**

My alarm clock rang very loudly. **(adverb phrase)**

We got ready for school as the sun was rising.
(adverb clause)

Because the bus got stuck in snow, we were all late.
(adverb clause)

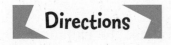 **Directions** On the blank in front of each group of words, label each adverb phrase with a "P." Label each adverb clause with a "C." The first one has been done for you.

_____C_____ 1. after the horse leaped over the fence

_____ 2. very slowly and carefully

_____ 3. if Marco doesn't arrive soon

_____ 4. although no one saw her

_____ 5. extremely quickly

_____ 6. while I was waiting for my friend

© Houghton Mifflin Harcourt Publishing Company

_____ **7.** so thankfully

_____ **8.** quietly and patiently

_____ **9.** before it started to rain

_____ **10.** because he finished second in the race

_____ **11.** not too well

_____ **12.** as the game was ending

> **Directions** In the sentences below, circle all the adverb phrases and underline all the adverb clauses.

1. My grandfather was feeling (very poorly,) so he stayed home.

2. Although they wanted a puppy, their mother was allergic to dog hair.

3. Get outside and play while the sun is shining.

4. Jimmy looked at me strangely and confusedly when I tried to explain the problem.

5. If nobody else wants the tickets, I'll take them.

6. She waited quietly and patiently for her turn.

7. Before the team ran out on the field, the coach gave them a pep talk.

8. We enjoyed the parade although it was very cold.

Next Step Write a paragraph describing a time you achieved something you are proud of. In your paragraph, use at least two adverb phrases and two adverb clauses. Read your finished paragraph aloud to a classmate. Have him or her identify each adverb phrase and clause.

© Houghton Mifflin Harcourt Publishing Company

Phrases and Clauses 4

An **adjective phrase** is a group of related words, lacking either a subject or predicate (or both), that modifies a noun or a pronoun. An **adjective clause** is a dependent clause that modifies a noun or a pronoun. Adjective clauses are formed using relative pronouns. (See 700.2 and 706.3 in *Write Source* to review relative pronouns and adjective clauses.)

Examples

It's good to see Andy wearing sunscreen. (adjective phrase)

The zoo animals at feeding time were very loud and boisterous. (adjective phrase)

We really liked the woman whom we met at the zoo. (adjective clause)

The zoo is the place where she learned about monkeys. (adjective clause)

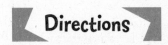 **Directions** On the blank in front of each group of words, label each adjective phrase with a "P." Label each adjective clause with a "C." The first one has been done for you.

_____C_____ **1.** who never worked a day in his life

_____ **2.** black, yellow, and red

_____ **3.** when Mom came home from the hospital

_____ **4.** that I saw in the program

_____ **5.** whose father is a firefighter

_____ **6.** carrying a bright green purse

_____ **7.** which I hoped was done cooking

_____ **8.** where all my friends like to meet

© Houghton Mifflin Harcourt Publishing Company

_____ **9.** soft and low

_____ **10.** that everyone enjoys

_____ **11.** who says he didn't see a thing

_____ **12.** cheering for the home team

_____ **13.** that broke the day I got it

_____ **14.** whom everyone admired

_____ **15.** rather obnoxious

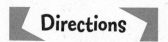 **Directions** In the sentences below, circle all the adjective phrases and underline all the adjective clauses.

1. I really want a guitar, <u>which costs more than I can afford</u>.

2. We all laughed at his extremely funny joke.

3. My cousin Ricardo, who wants to meet Maria, is coming to visit on Saturday.

4. I noticed the girl reading a book in the corner.

5. I showed off the mountain bike that I won at the raffle.

6. I knew my brother Jeremy, who practiced really hard, would win the contest.

7. The game that I want goes on sale on Friday.

8. The movie, which we saw on Friday, was a run-of-the-mill romantic comedy.

Next Step Write a paragraph about a visit you have made to a zoo, museum, or other interesting place. In your paragraph, use at least two adjective phrases and two adjective clauses. Switch papers with a classmate, and identify each adjective phrase and clause in your partner's paragraph.

© Houghton Mifflin Harcourt Publishing Company

Transitions

Transitions or linking words such as *finally, besides, however,* and *also* are used to connect ideas within or between sentences. In a long or complicated passage, transitions can also map out a pattern or structure for the reader to follow. (Refer to pages 572–573 in *Write Source* for a list of transitions.)

 **Directions** Use the following transitions to fill in the blanks in the paragraphs below. (*Note:* Some transition words should be followed by commas.) The first one has been done for you.

as soon as	**finally**	**before**	**when**
whenever	**in addition**	**in fact**	**after**

1   Video games are fun to play on a rainy day. In fact, I like playing these

2   games almost any time. _____*When*_____ the weather is good, no video game

3   can compare to playing baseball with my friends. _____ school is

4   out, we drop our books at home and head to the park. _____ we

5   start the game, we choose two captains who choose teams. _____,

6   we switch around so the teams are always changing.

7   _____ there is a close call (is someone safe or out?), everyone

8   starts yelling back and forth, but no one stays mad. Soon we are back

9   playing the game. Some days we play nonstop until it gets dark. When we

10 can't see the ball anymore, we know it's time to quit. _____, our

11 cell phones start ringing. Hank usually gets the first call. _____

that happens, the rest of us know it's time to head for home.

Next Step Write a paragraph explaining your feelings about computers. Use transition words to aid in clarifying your ideas. Read your paragraph aloud to a classmate.

© Houghton Mifflin Harcourt Publishing Company

Paragraph-to-Paragraph Coherence

Transitions are also used to connect paragraphs. Transition words and phrases can be used to link an idea in one paragraph to another idea in the next paragraph, helping readers understand how your ideas are related. Transitions also show how you are expanding on an idea introduced in a previous paragraph. Using transitions to connect your paragraphs can make the themes, patterns, and structures in your writing clear to your audience.

Here are some common words and phrases that can help you create paragraph-to-paragraph coherence. Most transitions require a comma when they come at the beginning of a sentence.

Moreover	As you can see	However	Similarly
In conclusion	Therefore	Next	Likewise
So	Another . . .		

> **Directions**   Use transitions from the list above to fill in the blanks in the paragraphs below. The first one has been done for you.

Choosing a guitar can seem like a major challenge, but there's an easy way to go about it. How? Ask yourself a series of questions. In answering them, you'll get a much better idea of which guitar to buy. The first question is, what kind of music do you want to play? Rock, blues, and jazz require volume, and for volume, you're looking at an electric guitar and amplifier.

_____*However*_____, folk musicians don't need the volume because they don't usually compete with drums and other loud instruments. If you want to play folk music, an acoustic guitar will suffice.

_____, students of the classical guitar should choose an acoustic instrument, preferably one with nylon strings. Almost all

© Houghton Mifflin Harcourt Publishing Company

classical music for the guitar is intended to be played on the softer-sounding Spanish, or classical, guitar.

_____, you need to know what kind of music you want to play. Do you want to play like Eric Clapton, B.B. King, Doc Watson, or Andres Segovia? Once you're sure about that, it's on to question number two.

_____, ask yourself how much you want to spend. Guitars can be very expensive; but remember that cheap guitars are harder to play and don't sound as good as better ones. It's easy to get frustrated if your guitar is incapable of producing a good sound.

_____, spending some money on a guitar can make you feel like you've made a commitment—which is a good thing! You won't want that money to be wasted, so you'll probably be more devoted to practicing.

_____, signing up for lessons will help you develop discipline. Knowing you've got to learn certain things before your next lesson—think of it as a kind of homework—can help you stick to it and put in the hours needed to get better.

_____, knowing what your guitar-playing goals are can help you get started on the right foot. Ask yourself these important questions before you begin. You'll be glad you did.

Next Step Choose a multi-paragraph essay you've written. Revise it to improve your paragraph-to-paragraph coherence by including transitions that link the paragraphs.

© Houghton Mifflin Harcourt Publishing Company

Sentence Fragments 1

A sentence fragment may look and sound like a sentence, but it isn't. It is a group of words that is missing either a subject or a verb or that doesn't express a complete thought. (See pages 502–503 in *Write Source* for examples of this type of sentence error.)

Examples

Sentence Fragment:

Also commonly referred to as seas.

Corrected Sentence:

Oceans are **also commonly referred to as seas.**

(A subject and a verb have been added to make this a sentence.)

> **Directions**   Some of the following groups of words are sentences, and some are not. Write an "S" on the line before each sentence; write an "F" before each fragment. Correct the fragments.

_____ **F** **1.**  ~~Covering~~ *Oceans cover* more than 70 percent of the world's surface.

_____ **2.** Oceans maintain the earth's climate by regulating air temperature.

_____ **3.** Supplying moisture for rain.

_____ **4.** The Pacific Ocean, by far the largest individual ocean.

_____ **5.** The Pacific covers nearly a third of the earth's surface.

_____ **6.** It is also the deepest ocean, with an average depth of 12,900 feet.

_____ **7.** Every natural element found in the water of the oceans.

_____ **8.** Evaporation, which removes freshwater from the oceans, leaving the salt behind.

_____ **9.** Rain returns freshwater to the oceans.

_____ **10.** Currents running through the seas like giant rivers.

© Houghton Mifflin Harcourt Publishing Company

Sentence Fragments 2

A sentence fragment is not a complete sentence. This group of words may look like a sentence, but it is missing a subject or a verb or is an incomplete thought. (See pages 502–503 in *Write Source*.)

Examples

Sentence Fragment: **Slept curled up on the rug.** (no subject)

Complete Sentence: **The dog slept curled up on the rug.** (A subject is added.)

Sentence Fragment: **The crow sitting in the tree.** (no verb)

Complete Sentence: **The crow sitting in the tree squawked.** (A verb is added.)

Sentence Fragment: **Not a good idea.** (no subject or verb)

Complete Sentence: **Pulling a dog's tail is not a good idea.**

(A subject "pulling a dog's tail" and a verb "is" are added.)

Directions

On the lines provided, write an "S" if the fragment needs a subject, a "V" if it needs a verb, or a "B" if it needs both a subject and a verb. Then choose from the list of possible answers in the column at the left to turn the fragment into a sentence.

Subjects and verbs
Kittens are
Barked
Cats had
Ran
~~**Is tired**~~
The dog
Cats have
Herding dogs

_V_ **1.** The dog running after the stick ⌃*is tired*.

____ **2.** Chased a flying disk through the yard.

____ **3.** Across the field and around the birdhouse, the crazy cat.

____ **4.** Find and herd cattle and sheep out in fields.

____ **5.** Good hearing, a keen sense of smell, and great night vision.

____ **6.** Born blind, deaf, and helpless.

____ **7.** After hearing the strange noise, the dog.

____ **8.** Their pictures on ancient Greek coins.

© Houghton Mifflin Harcourt Publishing Company

Directions Each would-be sentence below does not express a complete thought. Add words or phrases so that these fragments become complete sentences. (Rewrite the sentences on the line if necessary.)

1. Dogs and cats in the same household.

_____

2. People who like dogs are.

_____

3. Why dogs howl at the moon.

_____

4. Unless the dog is trained to heel.

_____

5. Our cat and her toy mouse.

_____

6. Because cats would stay out all night.

_____

7. Which is probably why a dog scratches its ears.

_____

8. Where most house cats enjoy hanging out.

_____

9. The dog and her puppies.

_____

Next Step Next time you are with a group of people, listen to them talk. See if they use more complete sentences or more sentence fragments when they speak.

© Houghton Mifflin Harcourt Publishing Company

Comma Splices

A comma splice happens when two sentences are connected with only a comma. They should be joined with a comma and a coordinating conjunction (*and, but or, nor, for, so, yet*), joined by a semicolon, or made into two separate sentences. (See page 504 in *Write Source* for more information.)

Example

Comma Splice:
Eating healthful food is good, sometimes you just crave junk food.

Corrected Sentence:
Eating healthful food is good **,** **but** sometimes you just crave junk food.

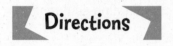 **Directions** Fix each comma splice by adding a connecting word ("and," "but," "or," "nor," "for," "so," "yet"), replacing the comma with a semicolon, or breaking the sentence into two sentences. The first one has been done for you.

1. Many foods that are labeled "natural" are full of sugar and salt, *and* some "low-fat" foods have unhealthy ingredients.

2. Air-popped popcorn is fluffy and white, movie-theater popcorn is soggy and yellow.

3. Candy bars taste better than energy bars, both kinds of bars give you an energy boost.

4. There are regular, no-fat, and low-fat potato chips, the tastiest potato chips are flavored with barbecue, sour cream, and onions.

5. Flour is the main ingredient in bread, rolls, and English muffins, it is also a major ingredient in cakes, donuts, and pies.

6. Some people think pizza is a fattening food, it definitely can be.

© Houghton Mifflin Harcourt Publishing Company

Run-Ons

A run-on sentence happens when two sentences run together without punctuation or without a comma and a connecting word (coordinating conjunction). (See page 504 in *Write Source* for more information.)

Example

Run-On Sentence:
My grandfather ate unhealthy foods all of his life he lived to be 91.

Corrected Sentence:
My grandfather ate unhealthy foods all of his life, but he lived to be 91.

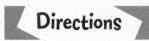 **Directions** Correct each run-on sentence below by making it into either two sentences (add end punctuation) or one sentence (add a semicolon or add a comma and a coordinating conjunction). Try to correct at least half of the run-ons by adding a comma and a coordinating conjunction. The first one has been done for you.

1. Corn syrup is found in soft drinks and candy bars, *and* it is high in calories.

2. There's corn syrup and high-fructose corn syrup I don't know the difference.

3. I do know that corn syrup contains dextrin, maltose, and dextrose I also know that corn syrup comes from the hydrolysis of cornstarch.

4. Hydrolysis sounds like a chemical process it must be helpful.

5. I'm still not sure what corn syrup is I don't know anything about dextrin.

6. Corn syrup tastes good it is sometimes cheaper to use than regular sugar.

7. I know what is in "100 percent fruit juice" maybe that's what I will drink.

8. My brother drinks only bottled water he says it has no additives.

Next Step Write several sentences about the ingredients in one of your favorite snack foods or desserts. Don't use any punctuation marks or connecting words. Have a friend do the same thing. Exchange papers and correct each other's run-on sentences.

© Houghton Mifflin Harcourt Publishing Company

Sentence Problems Review 1

It is important to present your ideas in clear, complete sentences. Sometimes errors appear in writing that make ideas hard to understand. Some of these errors are **sentence fragments, run-on sentences,** and **comma splices.** These sentence errors are easy to fix. (See the examples below and on pages 502–504 in *Write Source* for more information.)

Dr. W Dodge

Examples

Fragment:
If it leaked.

Complete:
If it leaked, it would sink.

Run-On
It leaked it sank.

Correct:
It leaked; it sank.

Comma Splice:
It leaked, it sank.

Correct:
It leaked. It sank.

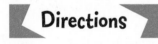 **Directions** ▶ Write "C" in front of a sentence that is correct, "CS" in front of a comma splice, "RO" in front of a run-on sentence, and "SF" in front of a sentence fragment. (The fragment example may also contain a complete sentence.) Then fix the sentence errors. One sentence will need two corrections. The first one has been done for you.

_**SF**_ 1. The movie *Titanic* tells the story of the disaster. As seen by

one survivor.

_____ 2. Survivor Dr. Washington Dodge of San Francisco reported his

observations of the wreck. Giving details in a 1912 newspaper story.

_____ 3. We had retired to our stateroom, the noise of the collision was not

at all alarming.

_____ 4. They started to lower the lifeboats after a lapse of some minutes

there was little excitement.

© Houghton Mifflin Harcourt Publishing Company

_____ **5.** The passengers were constantly being assured that there was no danger, as a matter of extra precaution, the women and children were placed in the lifeboats.

_____ **6.** I believe there were 20 boats lowered away altogether the excitement began after the sixth or seventh boat was launched.

_____ **7.** Some of the passengers fought with such desperation to get into the lifeboats that the officers threatened to shoot them.

_____ **8.** The starboard side of the _Titanic_ struck the big berg, the ice soon piled up on the deck.

_____ **9.** None of us had the slightest realization that the ship had received its death wound.

_____ **10.** Mrs. Isidor Straus showed most admirable courage, she refused to leave her husband even though she was urged to get into a boat.

_____ **11.** The 13th boat was filled with 20 or 30 children and a few women everyone was trying to stay calm.

_____ **12.** When the boats were drawing away from the ship, people could hear the orchestra playing "Lead, Kindly Light," rockets were going up from the _Titanic_ in the wonderfully clear night, heroic husbands and fathers were waving and throwing kisses to their womenfolk in the receding lifeboats.

Next Step Write a short paragraph about the _Titanic_ or another tragedy you've heard or read about. As you write, do not put any punctuation marks or capital letters in any of the sentences. Exchange papers with a classmate; then insert the punctuation marks and capital letters where they belong.

© Houghton Mifflin Harcourt Publishing Company

Eliminating Wordy Sentences

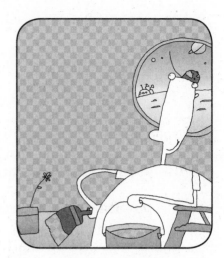

Resist the temptation to pad your writing with words and phrases that add nothing to the point you are trying to make. Also avoid expressions that sound good but seldom add anything worthwhile. (See page 506 in *Write Source*.)

Example

Incorrect Sentence:
The former tenant who had lived in the apartment before we moved in had painted all the walls with a coat of pink paint.

Correct Sentence:
The former tenant had painted all the walls pink.

 **Directions** Make the following sentences clearer. Cross out any unnecessary words or phrases. (Read carefully. Some sentences may sound fine at first even though they repeat ideas unnecessarily.) The first sentence has been done for you.

1. ~~As a general rule,~~ M/~~m~~ost of the new submarines ~~that were just purchased~~ are atomic powered.

2. The canceled flight has been rescheduled for 5:15 p.m. tomorrow evening.

3. He arrived there in Terre Haute yesterday morning at 7:00 a.m. and told us a humorous story about his trip that was very funny.

4. The very fast race car lapped all of the other cars that were in the race and made it look as if it were easy to do.

5. There are five people who want to drive in their cars to Sarah's house after the movie is over.

6. The difficult math problem, which was not easy to understand, caused me to fail the math test with an *F*.

© Houghton Mifflin Harcourt Publishing Company

7. The crowded shopping mall, which was filled to the brim with people, was evacuated at exactly 8:15 p.m. sharp.

8. The detective failed to solve the case because he didn't look for clues or spend time studying things at the scene of the crime.

9. He usually spends about two hours of his time each day at his computer.

10. Despite the strong effort of our team to defeat the opponent and win the game, we came up short and just barely lost.

11. My brother he is taking bowling lessons at the bowling alley while my sister she is practicing her gymnastic routines.

12. In September, my favorite rock group will return again here to repeat their recent performance at Center Stadium.

13. The movie's final ending caught me by surprise because I didn't expect it.

14. After we had finished the chores that we worked on, my sister and I rushed in a hurry to the theater to see the new movie that was just released.

15. The road between Burlington and Elkhorn follows and bends along the winding White River, a river with many twists and turns.

Next Step Write freely and rapidly for 5 to 8 minutes about one of the following subjects (or a subject of your own choosing). Make every effort to write nonstop so that the ideas flow freely.

1. staying at a friend's house
2. the prettiest place I've ever seen
3. a narrow escape from trouble
4. the best pet I ever had

Next, see how wordy your freewriting is. Cross out every word or phrase that is not absolutely necessary. Also have a classmate check your paper for wordy passages.

© Houghton Mifflin Harcourt Publishing Company

Rambling Sentences

Just as you should correct any fragments, run-ons, or comma splices in your writing, you also should correct any rambling sentences. Using too many *and*'s or *but*'s could result in a pileup of ideas and confusion for your reader. (See page 505 in *Write Source* for more information.)

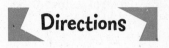 **Directions** Read the paragraphs below. Look and listen for sentences that ramble. Correct these sentences by taking out some (but not all) of the "and's," "but's," or "so's." Then correct the capitalization and punctuation as necessary.

1 Our student council wanted to help families in need in our community,

2 so we decided to have a canned-goods drive, but to do that, we needed to get

3 students involved on a "massive" scale, and that was no small challenge.

4 Our adviser, Miss Daniels, thought of starting a friendly competition

5 with each homeroom competing against the other homerooms, and one

6 homeroom at each grade level would win not only recognition in the

7 newspaper but also a pizza party.

8 Mr. Brzinski's homeroom began the food drive by bringing in the first

9 canned goods, and then Ms. Maher's homeroom got in the act, and before we

10 knew it, all the homerooms were involved, and for the next two weeks,

11 students were mowing lawns and baby-sitting, and buying canned goods,

12 and adding to each homeroom's total. We announced the totals at the end of

13 each day and stacked the cans on the stage in the gymnasium so all of the

14 students could see their homeroom's progress.

15 To say the least, we were more than pleased with the results, and the

16 newspaper took pictures of the huge piles of cans, and, most importantly, we

17 knew that we had helped many people, and that was the best reward of all.

© Houghton Mifflin Harcourt Publishing Company

Double Negatives

Adverbs describe the action of verbs. They also modify adjectives or other adverbs. Because they are so versatile, writers use adverbs frequently . . . and young writers often end up misusing them.

Using **double negatives** is an adverb-related problem that occurs when two negatives are used where only one is needed. Double negatives are grammatically incorrect according to the rules governing standard English. **Note:** Do not use *barely, hardly,* or *scarcely* with a negative word. (See page 510 in *Write Source*.)

Example

Double Negative:

Mom wanted to rent a cabin, but she doesn't **like** nothing **dirty.**

Corrected:

Mom wanted to rent a cabin, but she doesn't **like** anything **dirty.**

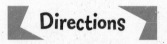 **Directions** Underline the double negatives in the following sentences. Then rewrite the sentences correctly. The first one has been done for you.

1. There <u>wasn't</u> <u>no</u> place without dirt.

   There wasn't any place without dirt.

2. We weren't barely through the door when we choked on dust.

   _____

3. There wasn't no sign of light in the cabin, so we started washing windows.

   _____

4. Mom never has no rival when it comes to cleaning.

   _____

5. By afternoon, there wasn't scarcely a speck of dirt anywhere.

   _____

6. Next year, we won't rent no cabin for a vacation; we'll take a cruise.

   _____

© Houghton Mifflin Harcourt Publishing Company

Misplaced Modifiers

Making certain your sentences are clear is a critical part of writing well. **Misplaced modifiers** occur when a modifying word or phrase is placed too far away from the word it modifies in the sentence. When that happens, either the modifier seems to modify a word that it cannot sensibly modify, or it is left without any word to modify at all. (For more information, see page 507 in *Write Source*.)

Example

Misplaced Modifier:

People driving a car with long hair **should keep their windows closed.**

(The sentence incorrectly states that the car has long hair.)

Corrected Version:

People with long hair **should keep their windows closed while driving a car.**

(It is now clear that it is people who have long hair.)

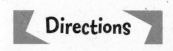 **Directions** Rewrite each of the sentences below. Correct the errors in modifiers by moving the modifier closer to the word it should modify or by adding or changing words in the sentence. The first sentence has been done for you.

1. The girl in the car with long blond hair waved at Alex.

    The girl with long blond hair waved at Alex from the car.

2. Screaming and shrieking, I discovered the boy running down the highway.

    _____

    _____

3. To make the team, coaches recommend that you practice long and hard.

    _____

    _____

© Houghton Mifflin Harcourt Publishing Company

4. I chased Dan as he jogged around the track on my scooter.

_____

_____

5. I could see Mrs. Smith trimming her flowers from the open doorway.

_____

_____

6. Hanging on for dear life, the bicycle crashed into the shrubbery.

_____

_____

7. Wandering down the hall, the baked chicken smelled wonderful.

_____

_____

8. To achieve good grades, teachers will tell you to listen carefully.

_____

_____

9. Buried under a pile of clothes, I found my old sweater.

_____

_____

Next Step Explain why a favorite fictional character from a book, a film, or a TV program appeals to you. Underline each modifying phrase you use and draw an arrow from the phrase to the word it modifies. Avoid any misplaced or dangling modifiers.

© Houghton Mifflin Harcourt Publishing Company

Pronoun Shifts and Double Subjects

Problems with pronouns can lead to confusing sentences. One common problem is a **pronoun shift.** A pronoun shift happens when a pronoun's person does not agree with its antecedent's person. (See 706.1 in *Write Source* for more about pronouns and person.)

Another problem to avoid is a **double subject.** This problem occurs whenever you use a pronoun immediately after the subject, which results in two words being used as the subject when you need only one. (See page 510 in *Write Source*.)

Examples

Pronoun Shift:

If <u>students</u> today complain about school, you should learn what schools were like after the Civil War.

("Students" is a third-person subject, so a third-person pronoun should be used.)

Corrected:

If <u>students</u> today complain about school, they should learn what schools were like after the Civil War.

Double Subject:

In the pioneer days, <u>children</u> they were often taught by their parents.

(The word "they" should be taken out.)

Corrected:

In the pioneer days, children were often taught by their parents.

 **Directions** Correct the pronoun shifts and double subjects in the following sentences by crossing out any incorrect pronouns. Write the correct form of the pronoun above each pronoun-shift error. The first sentence has been done for you.

1. In the country, a child ~~he~~ could walk several miles to *his* ~~your~~ school.

2. In the first public schools, children they went to school for 16 weeks or less.

3. Many country schools they had only one room for students of all ages.

© Houghton Mifflin Harcourt Publishing Company

4. A typical 30-by-35-foot school held 50 students in one room.

5. In newer city schools, two children shared a bench and a desk, and at exercise time, he flipped up the bench and exercised right by your desks.

6. Children in grades one through eight they exercised with a wand. The students waved sticklike wands, and by making patterns in the air, you developed your muscles.

7. Schoolbooks children used they were usually old and had no pictures.

8. Students had to buy our own books, and then we had to save them for our younger brothers and sisters.

9. Some parents thought that girls they should not go to school and that you should learn sewing and cooking at home.

10. Some doctors thought that if children spent too much time thinking in school, you could overwork your brains.

Next Step Describe schools today by finishing the three sentences below:
   1. In newer schools, children . . .
   2. In school, children exercise by . . .
   3. Students have to buy . . .

Add a second sentence using at least one pronoun for each example. (Be very careful not to have any pronoun shifts or double subjects.)

© Houghton Mifflin Harcourt Publishing Company

Sentence Problems Review 2

It is important to present your ideas in clear, concise sentences. Sometimes ideas are hard to understand because the sentences are wordy or ramble on. Try to avoid these kinds of sentences by writing about just one idea in each sentence and by eliminating extra words, especially *and*'s. Also avoid using too many short, choppy sentences. Combine them into smoother, more detailed sentences to make your writing clearer and easier to read.

 **Directions** Improve the following sentences by fixing rambling sentences, eliminating wordiness, and combining sentences. (*Note:* There are many acceptable ways to do this.) The first sentence has been done for you.

1 The sinking of the *Titanic* was one of the worst sea disasters ~~that~~

2 ~~happened at sea~~ in history. The luxurious British luxury liner left England

3 on its first voyage across the Atlantic and two days later the ship struck an

4 iceberg and sank and about 1,500 people died.

5 Work on the *Titanic* started with 15,000 workers in March 1909 and

6 work was completed on the ship's outside in May 1911. It took another 10

7 more months to finish the interiors of the ship and to add boilers, engines,

8 and four funnels, only the first three funnels were real. The fourth funnel

9 was a fake funnel added to make the ship look like it was larger and faster.

10 The *Titanic* was sailing across the Atlantic Ocean on its way to New

11 York City when it struck an iceberg just before midnight on April 14, 1912.

12 The ship sank in less than three hours. The *Titanic* was thought to be

13 unsinkable and many people believed it would not sink because it had 16

© Houghton Mifflin Harcourt Publishing Company

14   watertight compartments, but the iceberg punctured 5 or 6 of them. The

15   walls in the watertight compartments went only about halfway up the

16   ship's hull and water poured into the compartments and the water flowed

17   into the next compartment and it filled them up like water filling the

18   compartments in an ice-cube tray.

19   There were a number of reasons for the disaster. The ship had been

20   sailing too fast in dangerous waters and there were not enough lifeboats for

21   all the people and a nearby ship did not come to the rescue because its radio

22   was not on. The night of April 14 was clear and the water was calm and the

23   calm water made no waves and that made the iceberg difficult to see until it

24   was too late.

25   Believe it or not, the *Titanic* carried more lifeboats than were required

26   by law at the time in 1912. The *Titanic* was equipped with a total of 20

27   lifeboats that could carry a total of only around about 1,200 people. Many

28   people refused to get in the lifeboats they thought the *Titanic* passenger

29   ship was safe from sinking to the bottom of the sea and as a result, the

30   lifeboats went away with only about 650 people in them.

Next Step Read a newspaper article and look at the sentences. There will probably be few rambling or wordy sentences, but the sentence types and lengths may be similar. See if you can rewrite some of the sentences so they are more varied.

© Houghton Mifflin Harcourt Publishing Company

Subject-Verb Agreement 1

Subjects and verbs used together must agree in number. That is, they must both be singular or plural. In order to check for subject-verb agreement, you must first identify the main subject and its verb. Underlining the main subject once and the verb twice in your rough drafts will help you look for subject-verb agreement in your own writing. (See pages 508 and 509 in *Write Source* for help with special kinds of agreement problems.)

Examples

Rolfe studies **his paint job.**

("Rolfe" is a singular subject; "studies" is a singular verb.)

For a present-tense verb to agree with a plural subject (*birds, houses, children, geese,* and so on), the verb *must not end* in *s.*
The janitors study **Rolfe's painting mistake.**

("Janitors" is a plural subject; "study" is a plural present-tense verb.)
The janitors **from the district office** try **a new paint remover.**

("Janitors," not "office," is the plural subject. "Office" is the object of the preposition "from.")

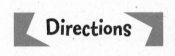 **Directions**

Underline the subject once and the verb twice in each of the following sentences. In the space provided, identify the subject and verb as singular "S" or plural "P." Don't be fooled by a prepositional phrase that comes between the subject and the verb. The verb must agree with the subject. The first sentence has been done for you.

_____*S*_____ **1.** The examiner tests at least 10 new drivers each day.

_____ **2.** Most new drivers appear very nervous before their tests.

_____ **3.** Examiners follow a checklist when testing.

_____ **4.** An older man, during his test, stops suddenly in the middle of a road.

_____ **5.** He then steps on the gas just as suddenly.

© Houghton Mifflin Harcourt Publishing Company

_____ 6. One nervous teenager searches frantically through his pockets for his car keys.

_____ 7. The examiner in the meantime examines his car.

_____ 8. Two happy new drivers leave the testing center with their licenses.

_____ 9. A middle-aged woman just misses another car in the parking lot.

_____ 10. She looks very nervous behind the wheel of her car.

Directions In a paragraph, recall an exciting or important event from one of your favorite books or movies. Use the present tense when you write to help make your paragraph exciting and interesting.

_____

_____

_____

_____

_____

_____

_____

_____

_____

_____

Next Step After you review your paragraph, read it aloud to a classmate. Then trade papers and check each other's work for subject-verb agreement errors.

© Houghton Mifflin Harcourt Publishing Company

Subject-Verb Agreement 2

Sometimes it is tricky getting subjects and verbs to agree. **Compound subjects** are double trouble when it comes to agreement. When a compound subject is joined by *and*, use a plural verb. If a compound subject is connected by *or* or *nor*, use a verb that agrees with the subject closest to the verb. (For more information, see pages 508–509 in *Write Source*.)

Examples

Jack and Jill were on their way down the hill.

(The subject "Jack" and "Jill" is plural so the plural verb "were" is used.)

Neither Jack nor Jill was able to avoid falling.

("Jill" is singular so the singular verb "was" is used.)

Jack's neighbor or his sisters were first on the scene.

("Sisters"—the subject closest to the verb—is plural so the plural verb "were" is used.)

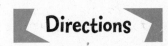 **Directions** Correct any errors in subject-verb agreement in the following sentences by changing the verbs. Do not change verbs that are correct. The first sentence has been done for you.

1. The owner of the well and his lawyer ~~says~~ *say* Jack and Jill were trespassing.

2. Jack and Jill testify that the well and the hill is unsafe.

3. Jack and Jill and their lawyer says the hill should be fenced off because it is too dangerous.

4. Then one lawyer or the other object, and the judge pounds his gavel to quiet the courtroom.

5. Jack or Jill need to ask permission and to pay for each pailful of water next time he or she goes to the well.

6. Jack and Jill say to forget it; they will drink bottled water.

Subject-Verb Agreement 3

When it comes to subject-verb agreement, **indefinite pronouns** can definitely be disagreeable and confusing. Some indefinite pronouns are singular. They act as singular subjects and use singular verbs. Singular indefinite pronouns are *another, anybody, anyone, anything, each, either, everybody, everyone, everything, neither, nobody, nothing, one, somebody, someone,* and *something.*

Some indefinite pronouns can be singular or plural—it depends on the noun they refer to. When the noun in a prepositional phrase following the indefinite pronoun is singular, use a singular verb. When that noun is plural, use a plural verb. These indefinite pronouns include *all, any, most, none,* and *some.* (See page 475 in *Write Source* for a chart and more information.)

Examples

<u>Anybody</u> who falls down a hill <u>is</u> in danger of being injured.

(As a subject, the singular pronoun "anybody" needs the singular verb "is.")

Luckily, <u>all</u> of the water in the pail <u>was saved</u>.

(Since "water" is singular, the pronoun subject "all" is singular, requiring the singular verb "was.")

<u>All</u> of the water bugs in the pail <u>were</u> not <u>saved</u>.

(Since "bugs" is plural, the pronoun subject "all" is plural, requiring the plural verb "were.")

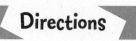 **Directions**   Correct any errors in subject-verb agreement in the following sentences by changing the verbs.

1. Neither Jack's parents nor Jill's mother ~~carry~~ *carries* medical insurance.

2. Each of them ask the well's owner to pay the hospital bills.

3. None of the parties agrees, so they go to court.

4. According to Jack, some of the boards around the well was missing.

5. "No way," says the owner. "All of that wooden platform were there."

6. Everyone in the courtroom start talking to one another.

7. The jury reaches its verdict, and nobody are very happy with it.

8. Half of the medical bills is to be paid by the well's owner.

© Houghton Mifflin Harcourt Publishing Company

Subject-Verb Agreement Review

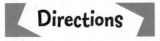 **Directions** In the following sentences, pick the correct verb forms to fit the subjects. Some subjects are singular, some are plural, some are compound subjects using "and" or "or," and some are indefinite pronouns.

1. Sara _____*likes*_____ middle school this year.
   (like, likes)

2. In all her classes, her teachers _____ great.
   (is, are)

3. Unlike last year, her classes _____ very challenging.
   (is, are)

4. During the noon hour, Sara and Beth _____ lunch together.
   (eats, eat)

5. Sara or Beth _____ dessert for both of them.
   (brings, bring)

6. Jermain _____ that this a good year for him, too.
   (thinks, think)

7. His friends _____ him how much fun he is.
   (tells, tell)

8. He _____ to learn as much as he can.
   (wants, want)

9. As always, Lydia _____ to do her best.
   (tries, try)

10. School and home chores _____ much of her time.
    (takes, take)

11. This year all of her classes _____ difficult.
    (is, are)

12. In shop class, Jermain's friend, Dillon, _____ very nice toys.
    (makes, make)

© Houghton Mifflin Harcourt Publishing Company

13. During the lunch period, Dillon or Lanny sometimes _____ these toys.
(sells, sell)

14. The money _____ for new shop equipment.
(is, are)

15. Shop students carefully _____ on their projects.
(works, work)

16. Each of the students _____ different materials.
(uses, use)

17. After school, Steve, Ron, and Herb _____ football.
(plays, play)

18. The basketball coaches _____ their players won't play football.
(hopes, hope)

19. For these coaches, tennis or swimming _____ fine.
(is, are)

20. Instead of playing other sports, some of the coaches _____ players
(wants, want)

to exercise.

21. Everyone _____ that high school will be even more fun than this year.
(says, say)

22. Our teachers _____ us quite a bit of homework.
(gives, give)

23. In high school, teachers _____ more homework.
(gives, give)

© Houghton Mifflin Harcourt Publishing Company

Combining Sentences Using Key Words

Ideas from two or three shorter sentences can be combined by moving a key word from one sentence to the other. A key word may be an adjective, an adverb, a compound adjective, or a participle.

Example

The pizza was just baked. + The cheese was bubbling. + The cheese was hot.

The cheese on the just-baked pizza was bubbling hot.

(In this example, three short sentences have been combined into one. Key words "just" and "baked" become a compound adjective. The key word "bubbling" is a participle.)

 **Directions** In each pair of sentences, underline the key word(s) in the second sentence and then move it to the first. The first one has been done for you.

1. Pizza dough can be tossed into the air. It should be tossed <u>gently</u>.

   Pizza dough can be tossed gently into the air.

2. Good pizzas are covered with cheese. The cheese should be gooey.

   _____

3. Peppers add color and taste to a cheese pizza. Red ones are colorful.

   _____

4. Mozzarella cheese is made from skim milk. The milk has no fat.

   _____

5. Those homemade pizzas were delicious. They were topped with pepperoni.

   _____

6. Pesto sauce looks strange on pizza. Pesto sauce is green.

   _____

© Houghton Mifflin Harcourt Publishing Company

7. Sometimes pizza tastes good for breakfast. The pizza should be cold.

_____

8. Many restaurants have Italian-sounding names. These restaurants serve pizza.

_____

9. The chef baked a pizza. He was singing.

_____

10. The pizza was too hot to eat. It was steaming.

_____

11. Pizza delivery people drive fast. They drive extremely fast.

_____

12. My brother got a job as a restaurant mascot. He got it Friday.

_____

_____

13. It is hot and smelly inside the mascot's costume. The costume is insulated.

_____

_____

14. The mascot waved to the children. The mascot was smiling.

_____

Next Step Write five short sentences using the following subjects: (1) The girl . . . (2) The boy . . . (3) The teacher . . . (4) The dog . . . (5) The monster . . . . Pair up your sentences with a classmate's. Then use key words to combine the sentence pairs. Don't worry if some of the new sentences don't seem very logical. The idea is to combine the sentences with key words.

© Houghton Mifflin Harcourt Publishing Company

Combining Sentences with a Series of Words or Phrases

Similar ideas from several short sentences can be combined into one sentence using a series of words or phrases. The words or phrases in a series should be stated in the same way (should be parallel) so that the sentence does not sound awkward. (See pages 512–513 in *Write Source* for more information.)

Example

The soccer fans were loud. They were rowdy. They destroyed things.
The soccer fans were loud, rowdy, **and** destructive.

(The words in the series are parallel. "Loud," "rowdy," and "destructive" are all adjectives.)

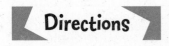 **Directions** Check off the words or phrases in each sentence below that will make each series parallel. The first one has been done for you. *Important Note:* The last item in the series is always correct.

1. At the start of the World Series, the crowd sang the national anthem

   ✔ loudly, ✔ proudly, ____ bad, and off-key.

2. The umpire yelled "Play ball" in a

   ____ not pleasant sounding, ____ loud, ____ raspy, and monotone voice.

3. The veteran pitcher was

   ____ winding up, ____ watching the catcher, ____ sneaky, and checking first base.

4. He fired a split-finger fastball that

   ____ curved in, ____ is doing funny things, ____ dropped off, and tailed away.

5. The batter hit the ball to the shortstop who

   ____ charged, ____ scooped, ____ jumped, and threw in time for the out.

© Houghton Mifflin Harcourt Publishing Company

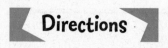

Directions Combine the ideas in the shorter sentences into one sentence that contains a series of parallel words or phrases. The first one has been done for you.

1. "That pitch was inside," argued the manager. "And it was high and tight."

   "That pitch was inside, high, and tight," argued the manager.

2. The announcer yelled, "That ball is going. It's still going. It's gone!"

   _____

3. The batter hit a home run. He hit a single and a triple, too.

   _____

4. The team's uniform has a red jersey. The cap is blue, and the pants are white and gray.

   _____

   _____

5. The old stadium has a crumbling wall. Its roof leaks, and its seats wobble.

   _____

6. The umpire called, "There's one ball. There's one strike. There's one out."

   _____

7. The relief pitcher scowled and stared. He kicked and threw.

   _____

8. That pitcher throws a blazing fastball. He has a sharp curveball. He also throws a sinking slider.

   _____

   _____

Next Step Think of a sports figure that you admire. Write a list of words that describe him or her. Combine three or more similar words in a parallel series and use the series in a sentence.

© Houghton Mifflin Harcourt Publishing Company

Combining Sentences with Compound Subjects and Predicates

By using compound subjects and predicates, you can combine ideas from shorter sentences into one sentence. A compound subject includes two or more subjects, and a compound predicate includes two or more verbs.

Examples

Two Shorter Sentences:
A moose ran through our campsite. A squirrel ran through our campsite.

Combined Sentence with Compound Subject:
A moose and a squirrel ran through our campsite.

Two Shorter Sentences:
The squirrel opened an acorn. It ate the acorn.

Combined Sentence with Compound Verb:
The squirrel opened and ate an acorn.

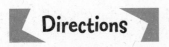 **Directions** Combine the following shorter sentences in each example into one sentence having a compound subject or a compound predicate.

1. Baby moose are called calves. Baby elk and cattle are called calves.

_____

2. A full-grown moose stands six feet tall. It weighs as much as 1,600 pounds.

_____

_____

3. A bull moose's antlers grow all summer. They can weigh 75 pounds.

_____

_____

© Houghton Mifflin Harcourt Publishing Company

4. Moose eat tree bark and twigs. Beavers eat twigs and bark.

   _____

5. Animals with four stomachs are called ruminants. Goats, deer, and cattle have four stomachs. Moose have four stomachs.

   _____

   _____

6. When the snow is deep, a moose will bite off a mouthful of bark. It will chew the bark. Then it will swallow it.

   _____

   _____

7. Moose flies are pests that bug moose during the summer. During the same time, blackflies and deerflies bother moose.

   _____

   _____

8. A moose can swim fast. A moose can run about 30 miles an hour.

   _____

9. Streams are good places to see moose. You can also see them in ponds and meadows.

   _____

   _____

10. An angry moose will charge you if it feels threatened. It could kick you. It could bite.

   _____

   _____

Next Step Look at a young child's storybook or picture book. See how many of its short sentences you can combine by creating compound subjects or predicates.

© Houghton Mifflin Harcourt Publishing Company

Kinds of Sentences 1

Sentences can be defined by the number and types of clauses they contain (*form*). Another way of defining sentences is by what they do (*function*). Each kind of sentence has a specific job to do and, based on that job, will use a specific kind of end punctuation. (For more information, see page 518 in *Write Source*.)

Examples

Declarative Sentence:

I write my e-mail on a laptop.

(A declarative sentence makes a statement about a person, a place, a thing, or an idea and ends with a period.)

Imperative Sentence:

Use the "power off" command to shut off the TV.

(An imperative sentence gives a command and often has an understood subject: "you.")

Exclamatory Sentence:

I got 20 e-mail messages in one day!

(An exclamatory sentence expresses strong emotion or surprise and ends with an exclamation point.)

Interrogative Sentence:

Did Uncle Steve answer your e-mail?

(An interrogative sentence asks a question and ends with a question mark.)

> **Directions**   Identify the sentences in the paragraph that follows. Decide the purpose of each sentence in the paragraph. Place a capital letter at the beginning of each sentence and then insert the correct punctuation mark at the end of the sentence. The first sentence has been done for you.

1   Last week we had a substitute English teacher for three days. her

2   name was Ms. Helms wow, was she nervous on her first day how did I

3   know she was nervous all I had to do was look at her hand when she

4   wrote on the blackboard her hand was shaking so badly she almost

5   dropped the chalk her voice squeaked when she tried to talk, and she

© Houghton Mifflin Harcourt Publishing Company

6   kept looking at the door as though she expected someone to arrive to

7   rescue her the entire class could feel her nervousness everyone in the

8   class tried to act normally to avoid upsetting her any more apparently

9   what we considered normal wasn't much help when Billy accidentally

10   dropped a book on the floor, Ms. Helms jumped about a foot straight

11   up in the air after she had gone, we discovered Ms. Helms had never

12   been in front of a class before the class was actually happy to hear

13   the familiar tones of our regular teacher when she returned after three

14   days at least we didn't have to worry about causing her to have a

15   nervous breakdown

Directions

Pretend that you are a substitute teacher in front of a class for the first time. Write about your experience using the four kinds of sentences below. You may put the sentences in any order, but be sure to use correct end punctuation. (Check each sentence off after you use it.)

☐ **Declarative**   ☐ **Imperative**   ☐ **Exclamatory**   ☐ **Interrogative**

_____

_____

_____

_____

_____

_____

_____

© Houghton Mifflin Harcourt Publishing Company

Kinds of Sentences 2

Sentences are classified by what they do (*function*). Some sentences make a statement (**declarative**); some ask a question (**interrogative**); some give a command (**imperative**); and some express strong emotion (**exclamatory**). Some sentences, especially imperative sentences, have understood subjects. (See page 518 in *Write Source* for more information.)

Example

Please <u>close</u> the door. (or) **Please <u>close</u> the door!**

("You" is the understood subject of these sentences.)

 **Directions** Place the proper punctuation at the end of each sentence below. Be sure to determine the function of the sentence based on the meaning and tone of the words. (*Note:* Some declarative and imperative sentences can become exclamatory sentences by using an exclamation point instead of a period.)

1 "Please close the door quickly "

2 "Should I lock it "

3 "Yes, and quickly "

4 "How do I lock it "

5 "Here, let me show you "

6 "Wow, don't close the door on my hand I need that hand to use the

7 periscope "

8 "Would I ever close the door on your hand "

9 "No, I would hope not "

10 "If anything like that ever happened, you'd know that it was an

11 accident "

12 "Of course "

© Houghton Mifflin Harcourt Publishing Company

Directions

In the space below, write a dialogue that might take place between two characters. The dialogue can be similar to the one in the previous exercise. Place proper punctuation—punctuation that fits the purpose of the sentence—at the end of each sentence.

_____

_____

_____

_____

_____

_____

_____

_____

_____

_____

_____

_____

_____

_____

_____

_____

_____

© Houghton Mifflin Harcourt Publishing Company

Types of Sentences 1

There are four basic types of sentences: **simple, compound, complex,** and **compound-complex.** Each type is determined by the number of clauses—as well as the kind of clauses—used in it. Remember, clauses can be either independent or dependent. An independent clause can stand alone as a sentence. A dependent clause cannot. (See 698.1–698.3 in *Write Source* for more information on clauses and pages 500–501 and 516–517 for information on sentence types.)

Examples

Simple Sentence:

John's story gave me goose bumps.

(one independent clause)

Compound Sentence:

John has a great imagination, and I always enjoy his writing.

(two or more independent clauses joined by a comma and a coordinating conjunction or joined by a semicolon)

Complex Sentence:

After John writes a story, he lets it "cool" for a few days.

(one independent clause and one or more dependent clauses)

Compound-Complex Sentence:

Although I do not write nearly as well as John, my writing is getting better, and extra work will improve it even more.

(two or more independent clauses and one or more dependent clauses)

Note: A simple sentence can have a compound subject or a compound verb. Do not confuse it with a compound sentence—a sentence that has two independent clauses.

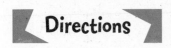 **Directions**   Read each sentence below carefully. Label each sentence type on the line ("simple," "compound," "complex," or "compound-complex"). The first one has been done for you.

_____*simple*_____ **1.** Dawn and Rose watched the concert on TV last night.

_____ **2.** It featured a reunion of The Eagles, and the singers looked really old.

© Houghton Mifflin Harcourt Publishing Company

_____ **3.** I wonder what today's singers will look like in 20 years; most of them will be older than my dad is now.

_____ **4.** It would be weird to see male singers with only as much hair as my dad has.

_____ **5.** My dad has a beard, and he always claims that the hair missing on his head just decided to grow on his face instead.

_____ **6.** Because he has had the beard for so long, I can't remember what he looked like without it.

_____ **7.** My dad with hair and young male singers without hair are equally hard to imagine.

_____ **8.** After I saw that concert, I decided not to watch any more TV reunion concerts for a while.

Directions

In the space provided below, write an example of each type of sentence. Try using your simple sentence as a base for the other, more complicated sentences.

1. (*simple*) _____

2. (*compound*) _____

_____

3. (*complex*) _____

_____

4. (*compound-complex*) _____

_____

_____

© Houghton Mifflin Harcourt Publishing Company

Types of Sentences 2

Sentences are categorized by how they are put together (*form*), and the form is determined by the type and number of clauses a sentence contains. How the clauses—dependent or independent—are combined determines the type of sentence. The four types of sentences are shown in the examples below. (Also see pages 500–500 and 516–517 in *Write Source*.)

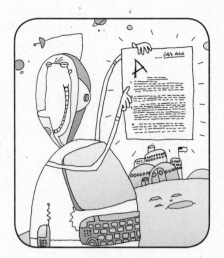

Examples

Simple Sentence:

I passed the English test with an "A."

(one independent clause)

Compound Sentence:

I passed the English test with an "A," and my parents were very happy.

I passed the English test with an "A"; my parents were very happy.

(two or more independent clauses joined by a comma and a coordinating conjunction or joined by a semicolon)

Complex Sentence:

When my parents are happy, I am happy.

(one independent clause and one or more dependent clauses)

Compound-Complex Sentence:

If I want to keep my parents happy, I should keep passing my English tests, and it might be a good idea to pass my math tests, too.

(two or more independent clauses and one or more dependent clauses)

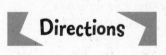 **Directions** For each sentence that follows, label its sentence type in the space provided ("simple," "compound," "complex," "compound-complex"). The first sentence has been done for you.

_____*complex*_____ **1.** My friend Bob is a fanatic when it comes to collecting comics.

_____ **2.** Bob puts each comic in a plastic cover and files all the comics in special boxes.

© Houghton Mifflin Harcourt Publishing Company

_____ **3.** He has been collecting comics for about three years now, and his collection takes up almost all the available space in his attic.

_____ **4.** He explained to me that the comics are very fragile and can easily be damaged if they aren't protected or if they are handled too much.

_____ **5.** The scarcity of a comic and its condition determine its value.

_____ **6.** The big event for Bob every year is the comic-book convention, Com-Con, in Chicago.

_____ **7.** His big thrill at the convention this year was talking to artists Frank Miller and Todd McFarlane and getting them to autograph copies of his comic books.

_____ **8.** Even though Bob has been offered quite a bit of money for some of his comics, he has never parted with a single one.

_____ **9.** Despite having to be so careful, Bob still loves reading his comics, and he also loves the whole process of searching for new additions to his collection, which is the thing I find hard to understand.

Next Step Clip a comic figure out of a newspaper and write a paragraph describing that character. Try to use a variety of sentence forms—*simple, compound, complex, compound-complex*—in your paragraph. When you have finished, read your paragraph to a friend and ask him or her to draw the character based on what they have read. If your friend draws a rough picture of your character and then can identify who it is, you are a success. If not, go back and add some details to your paragraph.

© Houghton Mifflin Harcourt Publishing Company

Compound and Complex Sentences

Ideas from two short sentences can be combined into a compound sentence or a complex sentence. A compound sentence is made up of two simple sentences joined by a comma and a coordinating conjunction (*and, but, or, nor, for, so, yet*) or by a semicolon.

A complex sentence is made up of one simple sentence (independent clause) and one or more subordinate clauses (dependent clauses). A subordinate clause may be introduced by a relative pronoun (*who, which, that, what,* and so on) or by a subordinating conjunction (*after, although, as, because,* and so on). (See pages 515–517 and 744.2 in *Write Source* for more information.)

Examples

Two Simple Sentences:
Many people play sports. Only the best athletes play professional sports.

One Compound Sentence:
Many people play sports, but only the best athletes play professional sports.

Two Simple Sentences:
Successful athletes talk to many people. They often inspire others.

One Complex Sentence:
Because successful athletes talk to many people, they often inspire others.

Directions Identify each of the following sentences as "compound" or "complex." Then underline the independent clause (simple sentence) in each sentence. Remember, compound sentences have two independent clauses. (*Note:* If you are unsure whether a word is a subordinating conjunction or not, you can look it up in a dictionary.)

_____*complex*_____ 1. Once you learn to quit, it becomes a habit.
—Vince Lombardi *(football coach)*

_____ 2. Before you can win a game, you have to not lose it.
—Chuck Noll *(football coach)*

_____ 3. If you can believe it, the mind can achieve it.
—Ronnie Lott *(football player)*

_____ 4. It's not the size of the dog in the fight, but it's the size of the fight in the dog.   —Archie Griffin *(football player)*

_____ 5. Winners never quit, and quitters never win.   —Unknown

© Houghton Mifflin Harcourt Publishing Company

_____ **6.** As long as the mind can envision the fact that you can do something, you can do it.
　　　　　　　　　　—Arnold Schwarzenegger *(actor / politician)*

_____ **7.** You show me a guy who's afraid to look bad, and I'll show you a guy you can beat every time.
　　　　　　　　　　—Lou Brock *(baseball player)*

_____ **8.** Everyone has limits on the time he can devote to exercise, and cross-training simply gives you the best return on your investment.　　—Paula Newby-Fraser *(triathlete)*

_____ **9.** Other people may not have had high expectations for me, but I had high expectations for myself.
　　　　　　　　　　—Shannon Miller *(gymnast)*

_____ **10.** When anyone tells me I can't do anything, I'm just not listening anymore.
　　　　　　　　　　—Florence Griffith-Joyner *(track athlete)*

_____ **11.** Whether I was in a slump or feeling badly or having trouble off the field, the only thing to do was keep swinging.　　　　　—Hank Aaron *(baseball player)*

_____ **12.** It's lack of faith that makes people afraid of meeting challenges, and I believed in myself.
　　　　　　　　　　—Muhammad Ali *(boxer)*

_____ **13.** If you don't do what's best for your body, you're the one who comes up on the short end.
　　　　　　　　　　—Julius Erving *(basketball player)*

_____ **14.** You need to play with supreme confidence, or else you'll lose again, and then losing becomes a habit.
　　　　　　　　　　—Joe Paterno *(football coach)*

© Houghton Mifflin Harcourt Publishing Company

Complex Sentences 1

Words like *after, although, before,* and *unless* carry a lot of meaning. They tell you when, how, and under what conditions the main action of a sentence happens. These words are **subordinating conjunctions,** and they are used to form complex sentences.

The group of words introduced by the subordinating conjunction is called an **adverb clause,** and it can come at the beginning or at the end of a sentence. This all sounds more complex than it is. The best way to understand adverb clauses is to see some examples. (See page 517 and 746.1 in *Write Source* and see the examples below.)

Examples

Chris made sure he had enough money. He bought a CD.
(Here are two short sentences.)

Before he bought a CD, **Chris made sure he had enough money.**
(The adverb clause is at the beginning of the sentence—a comma is needed.)

Chris made sure he had enough money before he bought a CD.
(The adverb clause is at the end of the sentence—no comma is needed.)

 **Directions** Combine the following short sentences into one sentence using the subordinating conjunction given in parentheses. The first one has been done for you.

1. I was only four years old. I started kindergarten. *(when)*

   I was only four years old when I started kindergarten. (or) When I was only four

   years old, I started kindergarten.

2. She checked her numbers. The woman realized she held a winning lottery ticket. *(as)*

   _____

   _____

© Houghton Mifflin Harcourt Publishing Company

3. I tried to stay calm. My heart was pounding. *(although)*

_____

_____

4. Kyna smiled innocently. She hadn't done anything wrong. *(as though)*

_____

_____

5. Bernadette felt lousy. She had lost her favorite necklace. *(because)*

_____

_____

6. Mark said he'd go to the party. He had to ask his parents' permission. *(use your own subordinating conjunction)*

_____

_____

7. I winced. I saw the math exam. *(your choice)*

_____

_____

8. Mom left a note on the door. Dad would know where we went. *(your choice)*

_____

Next Step Write a paragraph or two about what happened this morning between the time you got up and the time you got to school. Try to put in as much detail as you can. Then exchange your writing with a classmate. Note ideas in one another's work that could be combined using adverb clauses.

© Houghton Mifflin Harcourt Publishing Company

Complex Sentences 2

Too many "who's," "which's," and "that's" in your writing can make it sound wordy and impersonal. However, **relative pronouns** used in moderation can help you combine your ideas into more effective sentences. (The part of a complex sentence beginning with *who, which,* or *that* is called an **adjective clause**.) (See page 515 and 706.3, 710.1, and 746.1 in *Write Source* for more information.)

Examples

Simple Sentences:

The bookstore barely held all the people**. The** people **came to see Hank Aaron.**

("People" is unnecessarily repeated in these sentences.)

Combined Sentence:

The bookstore barely held all the people who came to see Hank Aaron.

(The repetition of "people" is avoided.)

Simple Sentences:

Aaron signed his book **called *I Had a Hammer*. The** book **had just been released.**

("Book" is unnecessarily repeated.)

Combined Sentence:

Aaron signed his book called *I Had a Hammer*, which had just been released.

(The repetition of "book" is avoided.)

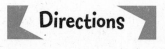 **Directions**   Study the two combined sentences above and determine why a comma is used in the second sentence and not in the first one. State your reason on the following lines. (Share your reason with a classmate. Then read the explanation of nonrestrictive phrases and clauses on 584.1 in *Write Source*.)

_____

_____

_____

_____

_____

_____

© Houghton Mifflin Harcourt Publishing Company

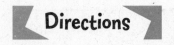 **Directions** Combine each pair of sentences below into one complex sentence using "who," "which," or "that" as connectors. *Note:* Key words and punctuation marks have already been put in place.

1. My dad talked about buying Hank Aaron's new autobiography. My dad enjoys reading about sports figures.

   My dad, who _____ ,

   talked _____ .

2. There was already a line when we arrived at the bookstore. That line went all the way around the block.

   There _____ that _____

   _____ bookstore.

3. We were in line for almost two hours. Two hours is a long time when you're hungry and there's no hot-dog stand in sight!

   We _____ ,

   which _____

   _____ sight!

4. Hank Aaron signed books continually. Hank Aaron stayed an hour longer than scheduled.

   Hank Aaron, who _____ ,

   _____ continually.

5. My dad was very disappointed. My dad never did get Hank Aaron's autograph.

   _____ , who _____ ,

   _____ disappointed.

Next Step Write a paragraph about someone you admire. Use relative pronouns to create complex sentences. Read your paragraph aloud to a classmate.

© Houghton Mifflin Harcourt Publishing Company

Sentence Expanding

What is it that keeps you reading a novel until midnight or trying to figure out *whodunit* in the latest movie thriller? It's the tantalizing details doled out in bits and pieces. Unpredictable, scary, or vivid—details make a story better.

Details often spill out of a writer's mind spontaneously. The writer might start with a brief sentence, attach a detail to it, tweak the wording a bit, tack on another detail, and so on. This is called **sentence expanding**. It allows a writer to be playful and vivid. Read the following examples and then try the exercise. (See page 519 in *Write Source* for more information.)

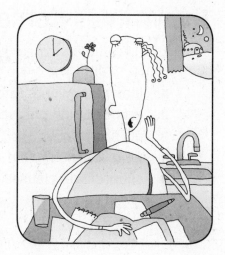

Examples

Start with a Basic Sentence:
Julie was studying.

First, we could say *when* Julie was studying:
Late last night, **Julie was studying.**

Second, we could say *where* Julie was studying:
Late last night, Julie was studying at the kitchen table.

Third, we could say *how* Julie was studying:
Late last night, Julie was studying at the kitchen table, memorizing terms.

Finally, we could say *why* Julie was studying:
Late last night, Julie was studying at the kitchen table, memorizing terms for tomorrow's science quiz.

Special Note: We could add more information, but the sentence as it now stands reads well. The point is to make a smooth-reading, interesting sentence, not a sentence that is piled too high with detail.

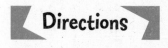 **Directions** | Now you try it. On your own paper, expand the following brief thoughts by adding details. Look for where these details might naturally fit—before, within, or after the basic sentence. (See "The Writer's Corner" on the next page for help.)

1. Roy slipped.
2. Ms. Rogers entered.
3. José swung.
4. Marcia turned.
5. The storm started.
6. A bear growled.

© Houghton Mifflin Harcourt Publishing Company

The Writer's Corner

Details come in a variety of shapes and sizes. Try to use the five different forms below when expanding basic sentences:

1. **individual words** (quietly)
2. **prepositional phrases** (at the kitchen table)
3. **participial** (*ing* or *ed*) **phrases** (memorizing a list of words)
4. ***who, which,* or *that* clauses** (who needed an *A*)
5. **subordinate clauses** (because the semester was almost over)

Let's try expanding the sentence "Roy slipped." How might you get started?

■ First, you could say *when* he slipped.

■ Second, you could say *where* he slipped.

■ Third, you could say *how* he slipped.

■ Fourth, you could say *why* he slipped. (This fourth element is optional. If your sentence already says enough, leave it alone.)

Next Step For more practice, write five of your own basic sentences. Then exchange them with a classmate and produce interesting expanded sentences from your partner's list. Compare your work with your classmate's. Make note of sentences you especially like in each other's work.

© Houghton Mifflin Harcourt Publishing Company

Expanding Sentences with Phrases

Readers expect a certain amount of substance and rhythm in a piece of writing. Their expectations aren't met if the writing is full of choppy sentences. That's why sentence-combining exercises can be so helpful. They give you practice producing sentences with enough body and form to keep readers interested in your ideas. See the examples below. (Also, see pages 519–520 in *Write Source* for additional explanations and examples.)

Examples

Infinitive Phrase:

I ran to see the first pitch.

("To see" is an infinitive phrase.)

Prepositional Phrase:

I ran to the bleachers.

("To the bleachers" is a prepositional phrase.)

Appositive Phrase:

I ran to the bleachers, my usual spot.

("My usual spot" is an appositive phrase renaming "bleachers.")

Participial Phrase:

Worried about being late, I ran to the bleachers.

("Worried about being late" is a participial phrase describing "I.")

Expanded Sentence:

Worried about being late, I ran to the bleachers, my usual spot, to see the first pitch.

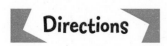 **Directions**   Combine each pair of short sentences using the type of phrase indicated in parentheses. (Share your results.)

1. I returned the stale chocolate bars. They had been purchased at Ralph's Candy Shack. (*participial phrase*)

_____

_____

© Houghton Mifflin Harcourt Publishing Company

2. We rode in the stretch limousine. It was the one with the gold-plated wheel covers. *(prepositional phrase)*

_____

_____

3. Jerome's idea doesn't surprise me at all. His idea is to run full speed into the ice-cold water. *(infinitive phrase)*

_____

_____

4. My neighbor took me for a short flight in his private plane. He is a commercial pilot. *(appositive phrase)*

_____

_____

5. My older brother already left. He left for his first guitar lesson. *(prepositional phrase)*

_____

_____

6. We made plans. Our plans were to surprise our teacher with a birthday party. *(infinitive phrase)*

_____

_____

7. The chapter is the one on photosynthesis. It is the one to read carefully. *(infinitive phrase)*

_____

_____

Next Step Spend 3 to 5 minutes writing about what you eat when you are really, really hungry. (You may exaggerate a little.) As you review your writing, combine ideas as necessary to help your sentences read more effectively. Then exchange "menus" with a classmate and see if there are any more of your partner's sentences you can combine.

© Houghton Mifflin Harcourt Publishing Company

Adding Style to Sentences

One of the easiest ways to add style and variety to writing is to use modifiers, phrases, and clauses at the beginnings of your sentences. If too many of your sentences start the same way—with the subject— your writing may begin to sound dull or flat. (See pages 511–522 in *Write Source* for help.)

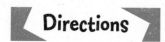 **Directions**
Each of the following sentences begins with a subject. Reword each sentence twice (use two different beginnings). You can use one-word modifiers, phrases, or clauses to start your revised sentences. (The subject in each sentence is highlighted in boldfaced type.) The first one has been done for you.

1. **Treasures** totaling billions of dollars are waiting across the United States for treasure hunters.

   a. *Across the United States, treasures totaling billions of dollars are waiting*

      for treasure hunters.

   b. *Waiting for treasure hunters across the United States are*

      treasures totaling billions of dollars.

2. **Gold mines,** overgrown and hidden by time, contain large fortunes in the western part of our country.

   a. _____

      _____

   b. _____

      _____

© Houghton Mifflin Harcourt Publishing Company

3. **People** distrustful of banks hid valuables that now remain unclaimed.

   a. _____

   _____

   b. _____

   _____

4. Treasure **hunters** searching for hot prospects read old newspapers and magazines while the rest of us work regular jobs.

   a. _____

   _____

   b. _____

   _____

5. Antique **dolls,** in addition to antique furniture, plates, and jewelry, are very valuable today because many people collect old and interesting objects.

   a. _____

   _____

   _____

   b. _____

   _____

   _____

6. The **tool** most valuable to a treasure hunter is his or her own mind, even though a good metal detector can come in handy.

   a. _____

   _____

   b. _____

   _____

© Houghton Mifflin Harcourt Publishing Company

Sentence Variety Review 1

Two important habits will help sentence combining have an effect on your writing. These practices are reading and writing on a regular basis. If you do that, you'll find sentence combining will begin making a difference in the way you write. (See pages 511–522 in *Write Source* for more information.)

Example

Simple Sentences:

Earl's father is taking a leave of absence. He has taught for 15 years. He teaches in a college. He will be writing a book.

Combined Sentence:

Earl's father, who has taught for 15 years in a college, is taking a leave of absence to write a book.

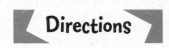 **Directions** Combine each set of simple sentences into longer, smoother-reading ones. Make use of all of the combining techniques you have previously worked on. The first one has been done for you.

1. The books were scattered.
   The books were for a science report.
   Magazines were also scattered.
   The magazines were for a science report.
   The books and magazines were scattered on Kim's desk.

   The books and magazines, which were scattered on Kim's desk,

   were for a science report.

2. The cafeteria was filled with laughter.
   The laughter was from students.
   The students were telling jokes.
   They were telling elephant jokes.

   _____

   _____

© Houghton Mifflin Harcourt Publishing Company

3. Fernando found the right kind of film.
   The film was for his 35-mm camera.

   _____

4. Fernando walked toward the checkout counter.
   He noticed a poorly dressed man.
   The man was standing next to a rack of candy bars.

   _____

   _____

5. The man carefully put some of the candy bars into his coat pocket.
   The man put them into his pocket while pretending to read a magazine.

   _____

   _____

6. Fernando saw him do this. He didn't know what to do.

   _____

   _____

7. The man obviously was trying to shoplift the candy.
   He looked like he was really down on his luck.

   _____

   _____

8. Fernando moved toward the checkout counter.
   A security guard came down the aisle.

   _____

   _____

Next Step Finish the story on your own paper. Exchange stories with a classmate. Find out how your partner developed the unfolding plot. Also note how effectively your partner combined ideas in his or her story.

© Houghton Mifflin Harcourt Publishing Company

Sentence Variety Review 2

Sentences can be combined with phrases, adverb clauses, or adjective clauses. You can use a series of words or phrases, compound subjects, compound verbs, and key words. You can also make complex and compound sentences. (See pages 511–522 in *Write Source* to review sentence-combining methods.)

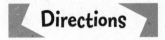 **Directions** In the following passage, combine some of the short sentences into longer, smoother ones. Use as many of the sentence-combining methods as you can. The passage below is a condensed, slightly rewritten version of a scene from *The Adventures of Tom Sawyer* by Mark Twain. (Copy the new sentences on your own paper if necessary.)

1   Tom appeared on the sidewalk. He carried a bucket of whitewash.

2   He carried a brush with a long handle. Tom looked at the fence. All

3   happiness left him. He sighed. He dipped the brush into the whitewash.

4   It passed over the top plank. He repeated the operation. He did it again

5   and again. Tom's energy did not last. He looked in his pocket. He got out his

6   worldly wealth and examined it. There was not much there. There was not

7   enough to pay another boy to paint the fence. It was a dark and hopeless

8   moment. An idea burst upon him! It was a great, magnificent idea.

9   He took up his brush and went to work. Ben Rogers came in sight.

10   He was eating an apple. He drew near. He slowed down. He stepped into

© Houghton Mifflin Harcourt Publishing Company

11 the middle of the street. Tom went on whitewashing. Tom looked at the

12 fence. He looked at it with the eye of an artist. Ben stared a moment. He

13 ranged up alongside Tom. Tom's mouth watered for the apple. He stuck to

14 his work. The brush continued to move. Ben watched every move. He was

15 more and more interested. He asked if he could paint the fence. He said he

16 would give Tom his apple. Tom gave up the brush. Ben worked and sweated

17 in the sun. Tom sat on a barrel and munched the apple.

18   Ben became tired. Tom traded the next chance to Billy Fisher for a

19 kite. Billy Fisher became tired. Johnny Miller bought in for a dead rat and

20 a string to swing it with. The middle of the afternoon came. Tom was rolling

21 in wealth. He had twelve marbles. He had a tin soldier. He had a dog collar.

22 He had the handle of a knife. He had had a nice idle time. The fence had

23 three coats of whitewash on it. He ran out of whitewash. If he

24 had had more whitewash, he would have bankrupted every boy in the

25 village.

Next Step Read chapter 2 of *The Adventures of Tom Sawyer*. See how your combined
sentences match up to Mark Twain's sentences.

© Houghton Mifflin Harcourt Publishing Company

Parts of Speech
Activities

Every activity includes a main practice section in which you learn about or review the different parts of speech. Most of the activities include helpful *Write Source* references. In addition, the **Next Step** activities give you follow-up practice with certain skills.

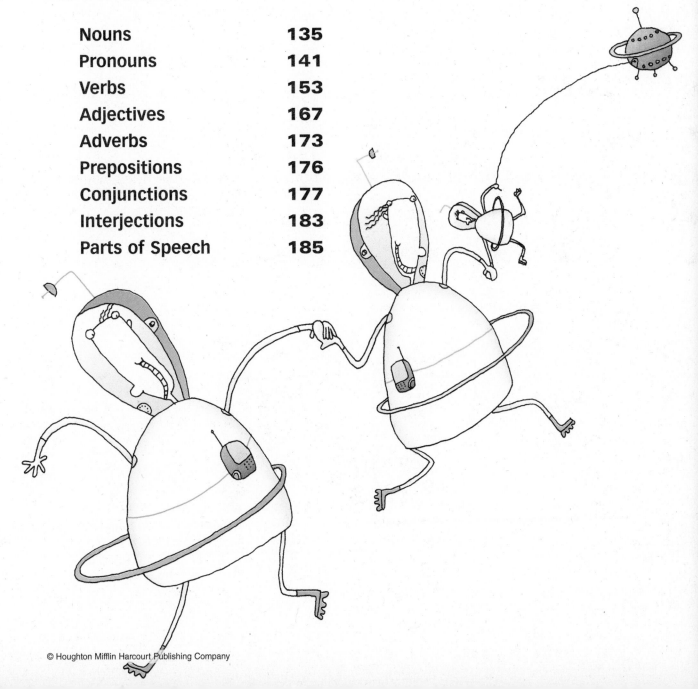

© Houghton Mifflin Harcourt Publishing Company

Concrete, Abstract, and Collective Nouns

A noun names either a person, a place, a thing, or an idea. Nouns can be sorted by what they name. A **concrete** noun names something that can be seen or touched. An **abstract** noun names something that you can think about, such as an idea or a feeling, but that you cannot see or touch. A **collective** noun names a collection or group of persons, animals, places, or things. (See pages 471 and 702 in *Write Source*.)

Examples

Concrete Nouns: student, cookie, Denmark

Abstract Nouns: poverty, courage, quality

Collective Nouns: class, batch, team

 **Directions** In front of each of the following words, write "C" for concrete noun, "A" for abstract noun, or "COL" for collective noun.

C	1. brick	A	12. peace	COL	23. team
A	2. pride	A	13. fear	A	24. freedom
COL	3. cluster	C	14. herd	C	25. bike
COL	4. Rocky Mountains	C	15. *Titanic*	C	26. water
C	5. snowboard	A	16. democracy	A	27. help
A	6. excellence	C	17. school	C	28. dog
C	7. computer	COL	18. United States	C	29. pizza
COL	8. bunch	COL	19. flock	COL	30. pack
COL	9. family	A	20. love	A	31. anger
COL	10. Green Bay Packers	C	21. tree	COL	32. group
A	11. happiness	A	22. religion	COL	33. litter

© Houghton Mifflin Harcourt Publishing Company

Directions Complete the sentences below, choosing some of your words from the previous list of concrete, abstract, and collective nouns.

1. My favorite sports team is the _Green Bay Packers_ .

2. I think our school needs more _pizza_ .

3. _My mom_ is a person I admire.

4. My friends and I could be called a _bunch_ of _people_ .

5. I would like to visit the _Rocky Mountains_ .

6. In my _family_ , we have a pet _dog_ .

7. _Freedom_ is something that I strongly believe in.

8. I could listen to the music of _Titanic_ all day.

9. If I lived on a farm, I would raise a _herd_ of _cows_ .

10. When I see _my dog_ , I feel _happy_ .

11. My most enjoyable day was _Friday_ .

12. In our _school_ , we have a strong sense of _peace_ .

13. On television, I like to watch _the news_ .

14. The emotion that best describes me is _love_ .

15. I would like to meet _the presidents_ at the _White House_ .

Pack of wolves
pride of lions

Next Step Write as many collective nouns as you can think of that name groups of animals. For example a "herd" of cattle. Check your answers using a dictionary.

© Houghton Mifflin Harcourt Publishing Company

Uses of Nouns

A noun can be the subject of a sentence, or it can be part of the predicate of a sentence. It can be possessive or can act as an object. (See 704.4–704.7 in *Write Source* for more information.)

Examples

Subject Noun:
A subject noun is the subject, the doer, or the noun being talked about in the sentence.
The fish jumped out of the lake.

Predicate Noun:
A predicate noun follows a form of the verb *be* (*is, are, was, were*) and renames the subject.
Swimming is a fun summertime activity.

Possessive Noun:
A possessive noun shows possession and contains an apostrophe.
The boat's engine stopped, so I had to paddle back.

Object Nouns:
The volleyball game was played in the sand.
- *Object of a Preposition:* The noun "sand" is an object of the preposition "in."

The setter bumped the ball.
- *Direct Object:* The noun "ball" is a direct object, which receives the action directly from the subject "setter."

The setter gave the spiker a good set.
- *Indirect Object:* The noun "spiker" is an indirect object, which indirectly receives the action. To have an indirect object in a sentence, there also must be a direct object. In this sentence, the direct object is "set."

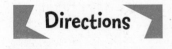 **Directions** For each underlined noun, write an "S" if it is the subject of the sentence, a "PN" if it is a predicate noun, a "POS" if it is a possessive noun, or an "O" if it is an object noun. The first one has been done for you.

PN 1. Summer is the best <u>time</u> for outdoor activities such as swimming and volleyball.

S 2. <u>Swimming</u> in a lake is different from swimming in a pool.

© Houghton Mifflin Harcourt Publishing Company

3. When swimming in a lake, you have to share the <u>water</u> with boaters, jet skiers, and people who fish.

4. When swimming in a pool on a hot summer <u>day</u>, you may find yourself sharing the water with the entire neighborhood.

5. A swimming <u>pool's</u> water temperature is usually warmer than a lake's.

6. Too many <u>bodies</u> in a pool make the water even warmer.

7. Swim goggles protect your <u>eyes</u> from the chlorine in a pool.

8. In a lake, you can wear a <u>mask</u>, fins, and a snorkel to see underwater.

9. Lifeguards at a pool or beach must be excellent <u>swimmers</u>.

10. They may have to give an injured <u>swimmer</u> first aid.

11. After a refreshing swim, a sandy beach is a great <u>place</u> to play volleyball.

12. Volleyball played with two people on each team is a fast-paced <u>game</u>.

13. It provides each team <u>member</u> plenty of exercise.

14. A <u>team's</u> success depends on how well the two players work together.

15. Each team usually uses all three <u>hits</u> to return a serve.

16. One player hits the ball high, so the second <u>player</u> can get under it.

17. The second player then sets the ball near the <u>net</u>.

18. The first player then charges in and spikes the <u>ball</u>.

19. After playing an <u>afternoon's</u> worth of beach volleyball, you can jump back in the lake and cool off.

Next Step Look over the exercise above. In the sentences marked with an "O," label the underlined nouns as either direct objects ("DO"), indirect objects ("IO"), or objects of prepositions ("OP"). *Write Source* can help you to decide which choice is best.

© Houghton Mifflin Harcourt Publishing Company

Nouns Review

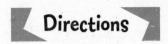 **Directions**   In the blanks below, list any common nouns that come to mind. (They are the ones that don't begin with capital letters.) But be quick. Try to show off your common k(noun)ledge by filling in the spaces in 3 to 5 minutes. (See 702.1 in *Write Source* for more information.)

Common K(noun)ledge

_____   _____

_____   _____

_____   _____

_____   _____

_____   _____

_____   _____

_____   _____

_____   _____

_____   _____

_____   _____

_____   _____

_____   _____

© Houghton Mifflin Harcourt Publishing Company

Get your "word's worth" in a poem.

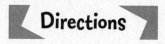 **Directions** Write a circle poem for one of the nouns in your list. (See page 359 in *Write Source* for an example.)

Next Step On your own paper, explain what is meant by the following types of nouns: *proper nouns, concrete nouns, abstract nouns,* and *collective nouns*. (Don't look in your book.) Share your explanations with a classmate. Then compare your explanations with those in *Write Source*.

© Houghton Mifflin Harcourt Publishing Company

Pronouns

Pronouns take the place of nouns and help make your writing read smoothly.

Example

Without Pronouns:
Tony woke up and thought that Tony would vary Tony's routine and ride Tony's bike to school.

With Pronouns:
Tony woke up and thought that he would vary his routine and ride his bike to school.

 **Directions** ▷ There are six kinds of pronouns covered below: personal, relative, indefinite, interrogative, demonstrative, and reflexive. See pages 706, 708, and 710 in *Write Source*. Then fill in the blanks below.

1. Personal pronouns take the place of _____ in a sentence.

2. An example of a singular personal pronoun would be _____ .

3. An example of a plural personal pronoun would be _____ .

4. An example of a reflexive pronoun would be _____ .

5. Three examples of relative pronouns would be _____ ,

    _____ , and _____ .

6. Three examples of indefinite pronouns would be _____ ,

    _____ , and _____ .

7. An _____ pronoun asks a question.

8. The four demonstrative pronouns in *Texas Write Source* are _____ ,

    _____ , _____ , and _____ .

© Houghton Mifflin Harcourt Publishing Company

Directions Underline all of the pronouns in the following selection. Then write the antecedent (the word the pronoun substitutes for) above each pronoun. The first few have been done for you. (*Note:* Indefinite pronouns such as *everything* or *anybody* do not have specific antecedents.)

1   Last week Mitch turned 17. After getting permission from his [Mitch's] parents,

2 Mitch bought his [Mitch's] first car. It [Car] was a lime green, 1975 Volkswagen Super

3 Beetle. When he brought it home, his parents were a bit surprised.

4   "I thought you were going to buy a truck," said his father.

5   "Well, this was cheaper, and I love the color," replied Mitch.

6   Mitch's father had owned a Beetle when Mitch was a baby, so they

7 decided to fix it up together. They gave it a good tune-up. Then they

8 checked its seat belts to make sure they were working properly.

9   "What should we do next?" asked Mitch.

10   "Since everything is fixed inside, we should wash the outside," said Dad.

11   So the Beetle, as dirty as city snow in March, was cleaned and polished

12 to a glowing green. With the roads clean and dry on an August day, Mitch

13 took his car for its first official spin. He went to the store to get milk for

14 his mom.

Next Step Read the selection to yourself, using only the antecedents, no pronouns. We think you'll see the need for pronouns here . . . and in your own writing.

© Houghton Mifflin Harcourt Publishing Company

Pronouns and Antecedents

A pronoun is used in place of a noun. The noun it refers to or replaces is called an **antecedent.** The antecedent usually comes before the pronoun. Pronouns must agree with their antecedents in number, person, and gender. When using pronouns, make sure that each pronoun-antecedent reference is clear, so readers are not confused. (See pages 476–477 and 706.1 in *Write Source* for more information.)

Example

The <u>detectives</u> solved the case. They found the missing money.
(The plural pronoun "they" refers back to the plural antecedent "detectives.")

Unclear Pronoun Reference:
The detective cornered the thief. He ran quickly down the alley.
(Who ran, the detective or the thief?)

Clear Pronoun Reference:
The detective cornered the thief, who ran quickly down the alley.
(Changing the pronoun "he" to "who" shows that the thief ran down the alley.)

 **Directions**   Write the antecedent for each underlined pronoun inside the parentheses following it. The first two sentences have been done for you.

1   Sam Slade and <u>his</u> (_____*Sam's*_____) partner, Millie Marlowe, were

2   in their office. It was a quiet morning, so <u>they</u> (___*Sam and Millie*___) started

3   cleaning up the place. Then the phone rang. <u>Its</u> (_____) loud

4   ring startled the pair.

5   "<u>I'll</u> (_____) get it," said Millie as she dashed to the phone

6   on <u>her</u> (_____) desk. "It's for <u>you</u> (_____), Sam."

7   Sam grabbed the phone and listened carefully for a few minutes.

© Houghton Mifflin Harcourt Publishing Company

8   He hung <u>it</u> (_____) up and sat on the edge of his

9   (_____) desk. "<u>We</u> (_____) have a case!" he

10   exclaimed. "That was <u>my</u> (_____) mom. Someone swiped the

11   chocolate chip cookies and <u>her</u> (_____) special secret recipe, the

12   one <u>she</u> (_____) used for the charity bake sale."

13   The two detectives hopped on <u>their</u> (_____) bikes.

14   "Let's rock and roll," yelled Sam.

15   "Race <u>you</u> (_____) there. <u>My</u> (_____) bike

16   is faster than yours," replied Millie, and off <u>they</u> (_____)

17   zoomed.

18   Millie's bike was faster, and she reached Sam's house first.

19   Sam's mom was waiting in the kitchen, and <u>she</u> (_____)

20   showed <u>them</u> (_____) a trail of cookie crumbs.

21   <u>It</u> (_____) led Sam and Millie to a closet door with a

22   chocolate-smeared handle.

23   They opened <u>it</u> (_____) and looked inside.

24   There sat the two thieves—Sam's brother, Sid, and Sid's friend,

25   Mick—with <u>their</u> (_____) faces stuffed with

26   chocolate chip cookies.

27   "I have <u>you</u> (_____) now," said Sam.

Next Step Sid and Mick surprise Mom. They make cookies for her while she is napping. A phone call interrupts them, and Sid has to take down a very complicated message. Write down the message that Sid took for Mom. Be sure that all pronouns agree with their antecedents.

© Houghton Mifflin Harcourt Publishing Company

Intensive and Reflexive Pronouns

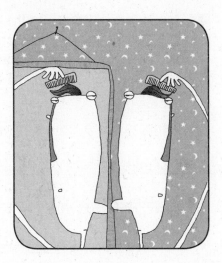

A **reflexive pronoun** acts like a mirror. It reflects back upon the subject of a sentence. An **intensive pronoun** emphasizes or intensifies the noun or pronoun it refers to. Writers use the intensive pronoun as a spotlight to focus attention on the antecedent (the word the intensive pronoun refers to). (See page 479 and 708.2–708.3 in *Write Source* for more information.)

Examples

Reflexive Pronoun:

The young man looked at himself in the mirror.

(The pronoun "himself" reflects back to the antecedent "man.")

Intensive Pronoun:

She herself never carries a mirror.

(The pronoun "herself" emphasizes or intensifies the antecedent "she." The sentence would still be complete if the intensive pronoun were taken away.)

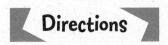 **Directions** On the seven blanks below, write a short sentence for each of the seven reflexive pronouns listed on page 710 in *Write Source*.

Reflexive Pronouns

1. _____

2. _____

3. _____

4. _____

5. _____

6. _____

7. _____

© Houghton Mifflin Harcourt Publishing Company

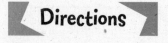

Directions On the following lines, finish the story started below. It's a story about a peacock named Narcissus. In your story, try to use all seven of the pronouns from *Write Source* (as reflexives or intensives). *Hint:* See what a dictionary says about Narcissus.

Once upon a time, there was a peacock who loved to look at himself in the

pond near his . . . _____

_____

_____

_____

_____

_____

_____

_____

_____

_____

_____

_____

_____

Next Step Exchange stories with a classmate. Circle each reflexive or intensive pronoun you find. Label each one "R" for reflexive or "I" for intensive.

© Houghton Mifflin Harcourt Publishing Company

Indefinite Pronouns

Words like *everybody, anybody,* and *everything* are **indefinite pronouns** that seem to talk about more than one person or more than one thing. They seem like plural words. But, in fact, pronouns ending in *body* (*everybody, somebody*), *thing* (*everything, nothing*), and *one* (*someone, no one*) function grammatically as singular words—as in "Everybody *has* a blank look on **her** (or **his**) face." (See pages 475 and 710 in *Write Source* for more information.)

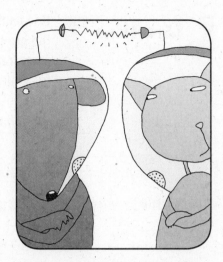

Directions　　Each of the sentences below contains an indefinite pronoun. Some of the verbs used with these pronouns are correct, and some are not. Underline each indefinite pronoun and change the verb or antecedent if necessary so that each sentence is clear and correct. The first one has been done for you.

　　　　　　　　　　　　　 his (or) her
1. Does <u>anybody</u> remember ~~their~~ first conversation with a pet?

2. Neither the dog nor the cat wants their ears examined.

3. Each of my friends has a pet.

4. Everything in the store's pet department are on sale.

5. Will someone please loan me and my dog their Frisbee?

6. Nearly half of all dogs likes to chase after sticks and balls.

7. Has anybody lost their box of dog treats?

8. Either my mother or my sister lost their grooming brush.

9. Something in our cat's favorite foods is good for tartar control.

10. Most of the food in our cat's diet are low-fat, yet tasty.

11. One of our cats like to sit and stare at the wall.

12. Nothing our cats do surprise me any more.

© Houghton Mifflin Harcourt Publishing Company

Directions

Use each of the following indefinite pronouns in a sentence. Underline the pronoun once and the verb twice. Be sure to use the correct singular or plural verb to go with each pronoun. The first one has been done for you.

1. none   *None of the students in my history class are going to the parade.*

_____

2. some   _____

_____

3. half   _____

_____

4. everyone   _____

_____

5. nothing   _____

_____

6. all   _____

_____

7. anything   _____

_____

8. nobody   _____

_____

9. one   _____

_____

10. each   _____

_____

© Houghton Mifflin Harcourt Publishing Company

Number and Person of Pronouns

When used in a sentence, personal pronouns have both a number and a person. (See 712.1–712.4 and the chart on the bottom of page 474 in *Write Source* for more information on the number and person of common pronouns.)

Examples

Pronoun Number:
A pronoun's number tells how many people or objects it refers to. The number can be either singular or plural. *You, your,* and *yours* may be singular or plural.

> **I volunteered to defend Boston from the British.** (singular)

> **We were given uniforms and taught to drill.** (plural)

Pronoun Person:
A pronoun's person tells who is making a statement, who is being spoken to, or whom the statement is about. A *first-person pronoun* takes the place of the speaker's name. A *second-person pronoun* refers to the person or thing spoken to. A *third-person pronoun* names the person or thing spoken about.

> **I saluted the commanding officer.** (first person)

> **You are a fine soldier.** (second person)

> **He handed the young recruit a drum.** (third person)

Directions For each underlined pronoun, write its number and person. Use an "S" for singular number and a "P" for plural. Use a "1" for first person, a "2" for second person, and a "3" for third person. The first sentence has been done for you.

_____P-1_____ **1.** About nine o'clock at night, <u>we</u> marched down to Breed's Hill.

_____ **2.** The British marched slowly, and <u>they</u> nearly reached our fort

when the battle began.

_____ **3.** This being my first battle, <u>I</u> remember great noise and much

confusion.

© Houghton Mifflin Harcourt Publishing Company

_____ **4.** Our sergeant said, "You are young and quick. Run and bring

back some medicine."

_____ **5.** "The major has been hurt, and he needs it quickly."

_____ **6.** When I returned to the hill, our men were confused, and they

were talking about retreat.

_____ **7.** I stayed with some others and covered the retreat until the

British were close at hand.

_____ **8.** They then took over our fort and four pieces of artillery.

_____ **9.** And to tell you the truth, very few of our reinforcements made

it in time.

_____ **10.** Then our orders came, and they said we were to make the best

retreat we could.

_____ **11.** We were tired, but we ran as fast as we could up Breed's Hill.

_____ **12.** I was exhausted by the time we reached the top, but we were

safe—at least for the moment.

Next Step Without looking at the definitions at the beginning of this activity, write
out your own explanation of the "number" and "person" of a pronoun. Use these words:
singular, plural, first person, second person, and *third person.*

© Houghton Mifflin Harcourt Publishing Company

Pronouns

151

Uses of Pronouns

In a sentence, a pronoun can be a subject pronoun, an object pronoun, or a possessive pronoun. (For more information about pronouns, see pages 706–714 in *Write Source*.)

Examples

Subject Pronoun:
A subject pronoun is the subject of the sentence.
After five years, I was still in the army.
(The pronoun "I" is a subject pronoun.)

Object Pronoun:
Following an action verb, an object pronoun can be a direct object or an indirect object. It can also be the object of a preposition.

I helped him buckle on his sword.
• *Direct Object:* (The pronoun "him" is a direct object.)

I never heard anything but good stories about him.
• *Object of the Preposition:* (The pronoun "him" is an object of a preposition.)

Possessive Pronoun:
A possessive pronoun shows ownership.
Meeting the general was one of my proudest moments.
(The pronoun "my" is a possessive pronoun.)

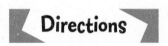 **Directions** Above each underlined pronoun, write an "S" if the pronoun is the subject, an "O" if it is an object, or a "P" if it is a possessive.

1   We arrived at the camp, and <u>we</u> were very anxious for battle. Night

2   came upon <u>us</u>, and General Morgan joked with <u>his</u> men. The next morning

3   was bitterly cold, and the men slapped <u>their</u> hands together to keep <u>them</u>

4   warm. About sunrise, the British advanced toward <u>our</u> position. <u>They</u>

5   shouted at us, and we yelled back at <u>them</u>. The general galloped by the

6   men and told them not to fire until <u>they</u> could see the whites of <u>their</u> eyes.

7   The British charged at <u>us</u> with bayonets, and we retreated. Just as we got

8   to our horses, <u>their</u> dragoons overtook <u>us</u>. But in a few moments, our

9   calvary attacked <u>them</u>, and <u>they</u> ran off. As both lines of infantry clashed,

10   the general ordered <u>me</u> to capture a British artillery piece. I saluted <u>him</u>

11   and charged with <u>my</u> men. <u>We</u> overran their position, and <u>it</u> was <u>ours</u>.

12   Now it was our job to use the artillery against <u>them</u>. The problem was

13   that <u>we</u> did not have any ammunition. So we decided the only way we could

14   get the cannonballs <u>we</u> needed was to collect <u>those</u> that had been shot at <u>us</u>

15   earlier.

16   We found cannonballs everywhere. <u>Some</u> were stuck halfway through

17   tree trunks. <u>Others</u> were buried under piles of rocks. Some were even

18   inside tents while others were mixed in with pots and pans. When <u>our</u>

19   scavenger hunt was over, <u>we</u> had gathered nearly 100 cannonballs. Now all

20   we needed was gunpowder and a target.

Next Step Write a paragraph about an activity that you do with a group (a sports team, a choir, a club, etc.). In the paragraph use the pronouns *I, me, my, we, us,* and *our.* Read your paragraph aloud to a classmate and ask him or her to listen for any incorrect pronoun use or unclear antecedents.

© Houghton Mifflin Harcourt Publishing Company

Simple Verb Tenses

Understanding the three simple tenses, or times, of a verb is not difficult. A verb is in either the **present** tense, the **past** tense, or the **future** tense. (For more information about verb tenses, see pages 482 and 720 in *Write Source*.)

Examples

Present Tense:
A present-tense verb expresses an action that is going on now or shows something that happens regularly.
People cross **the country using the same routes the pioneers used.**

Past Tense:
A past tense verb expresses an action that happened in the past. Many past tense verbs end in *ed*.
Pioneers crossed **the country in wagon trains.**

Future Tense:
A future tense verb states an action that will take place in the future. A helping verb (*will, shall, could*) helps a verb show the future tense.
You will cross **the country along a pioneer route if you follow Interstate 80.**

Directions Write the past and future tenses of the following verbs:

	Past	Future			Past	Future
1. is	was	will be	**8.**	crack	cracked	will crack
2. pour	poured	will pour	**9.**	move	moved	will move
3. drive	drove	will drive	**10.**	travel	traveled	will travel
4. start	started	will start	**11.**	swim	swam	will swim
5. eat	ate	will eat	**12.**	pay	paid	will pay
6. sound	sounded	will sound	**13.**	sell	sold	will sell
7. take	took	will take	**14.**	fly	flew	will fly

© Houghton Mifflin Harcourt Publishing Company

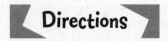 **Directions** Rewrite each sentence by changing the verb to the tenses listed. Change any other words as necessary. Keep the meaning of the new sentences as close to the original meaning as you can. The first sentences have been done for you.

1. It was four o'clock in the morning.

   Present It is four o'clock in the morning.

   Future It will be four o'clock in the morning.

2. People poured out of every wagon and tent.

   Present People pour out of every wagon & tent

   Future People will pour out of every wagon

3. Tomorrow the herders will drive 5,000 oxen into the corral.

   Present Today the herders are driving 5,000 oxen into the corral

   Past Yesterday the herders drove 5,000 oxen into the corral

4. The drivers pick their teams and hitch them to the wagons.

   Past The drivers picked their teams & hitched the wagons

   Future The drivers will pick their teams & will hitch them to the wagons

5. At six o'clock, we will eat breakfast and load the wagons.

   Present At six o'clock we eat breakfast & load wagons

   Past At six o'clock we ate breakfast & loaded the wagons

6. At seven o'clock, the 60 wagons will line up and then move out.

   Present At seven o'clock, the 60 wagons are lining up & moving out.

   Past At seven, the 60 wagons lined up & moved out.

Next Step Take a short passage from a book that is written in the present tense and rewrite it in the past or future tense.

© Houghton Mifflin Harcourt Publishing Company

Perfect Verb Tenses

It may take some practice, but you can understand perfect verb tenses. As with simple tenses, perfect tenses deal with time. (For more information, turn to page 483 and 724.1–724.3 in *Write Source*.)

Examples

Present Perfect Tense:

A present perfect verb shows action that began in the past and continues or is completed in the present.

Westerners have heard **tales of lost mines.**

(Add "has" or "have" to the past participle to form the present perfect tense.)

Past Perfect Tense:

A past perfect verb shows action that began and ended in the past.

Many prospectors had found **and then** had lost **valuable mines.**

(Add "had" to the past participle to form the past perfect tense.)

Future Perfect Tense:

A future perfect verb shows action that will begin and end in the future.

Mines yet to be found will have hidden **their treasures for centuries.**

(Add "shall have" or "will have" to the past participle to form the future perfect tense.)

> **Directions** List the past participles for the following present tense verbs. The first one has been done for you.

1. be ___*been*___

2. tell ___told___

3. feature ___featured___

4. uncover ___uncovered___

5. find ___found___

6. kill ___killed___

7. die ___died___

8. surface ___surfaced___

9. continue ___continued___

10. scour ___scoured___

11. unearth ___unearthed___

12. fight ___fought___

© Houghton Mifflin Harcourt Publishing Company

> **Directions** Use the past participles of the listed verbs with "have," "had," "has," and/or "will" to form the perfect tenses as shown. The first one has been done for you.

1. Over the years, Westerners _____*have told*_____ and retold many tales

   (*tell*)

   of lost gold and silver mines. (**present perfect**)

2. One popular story _____*features*_____ the legendary Lost Dutchman

   (*feature*)

   Mine in Arizona. (**present perfect**)

3. Along with three partners, a man known as Jake Miller ___*had found*___

   (*find*)

   the mine and left a map showing its location. (**past perfect**)

4. Miller ___*had killed*___ at least three people to keep the mine a secret,

   (*kill*)

   and many others ___*had died*___ trying to find it. (**past perfect**)

   (*die*)

5. Many legends about the mine ___*had surfaced*___ , including one story

   (*surface*)

   about Apaches filling the mine with rocks. (**past perfect**)

6. People ___*have continued*___ to search for the mysterious mine and its

   (*continue*)

   vast treasure of gold. (**present perfect**)

7. They ___*scour*___ the area south of the Salt River near Weaver's

   (*scour*)

   Needle and the Superstition Mountains. (**present perfect**)

8. If anyone finds the Lost Dutchman or other lost mine, he or she

   ___*will have unearthed*___ a long-hidden secret of the West. (**future perfect**)

   (*unearth*)

9. After many years of searching, the finder of a lost mine ___*will fight*___

   (*fight*)

   against terrific odds and won. (**future perfect**)

Next Step Write a paragraph about a historical topic in which you include present, past and future perfect tenses. Switch papers with a partner and find an example of each type of verb in your partner's paragraph.

© Houghton Mifflin Harcourt Publishing Company

Continuous Verb Tenses

Continuous tenses are yet another way to show time. Continuous tenses show actions that are taking place, will be taking place, or have been taking place at the same time as another action. All continuous tenses use a form of the verb *to be* and the main form of the verb + *ing*. (For more information, turn to 724.4–724.6 in *Write Source*.)

Examples

The **present continuous tense** shows an action that is continuing right now. It uses the present tense of the verb *to be (is)*.
Maria <u>is looking</u> for Alex's lost turtle.

The **past continuous tense** shows an action that was continuing at a specific time in the past when something else happened. It uses the past tense of the verb *to be (was)*.
Maria <u>was looking</u> for Alex's lost turtle when it started to rain.

The **future continuous tense** shows an action that will be continuing at a specific time in the future when something else will happen. It uses the future tense of the verb *to be (will be)*.
Maria <u>will be looking</u> for the turtle when the rain stops tonight.

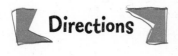 **Directions** Write "Pr" next to each sentence that uses the present continuous tense. Write "Pa" next to each sentence that uses the past continuous tense. Write "F" next to each sentence that uses the future continuous tense. Underline the verb in each sentence. The first one is done for you.

Pa **1.** I <u>was watching</u> TV when I heard the doorbell.

F **2.** Shana <u>will be playing</u> volleyball when the test is given.

Pa **3.** The wolf <u>was hunting</u> for food when the moon rose.

Pr **4.** He <u>is wondering</u> what your name is.

Pr **5.** The band <u>is practicing</u> on the football field.

© Houghton Mifflin Harcourt Publishing Company

158

_____F_____ **6.** We <u>will be listening</u> to the radio when the concert starts tonight.

_____Pr_____ **7.** You <u>are thinking</u> about my plan.

_____Pa_____ **8.** I <u>was planning</u> to go to the museum on Saturday.

> **Directions** Read each sentence. Fill in the blank with the correct continuous tense of the verb that is in parentheses. The first one is done for you.

are exercising **1.** Today, more people _____ (exercise) than ever before.

was reading **2.** I _____ (read) a brochure about fitness when Matt called.

was trying **3.** At the moment, he _____ (try) to decide which sport to try out for.

will join **4.** My friend and I _____ (join) an exercise class next week.

was singing **5.** The country star _____ (sing) the anthem when the power went off.

will play **6.** We _____ (play) football when the leaves begin to fall next month.

will perform **7.** The team _____ (perform) at a high level this season.

will root **8.** If we make the playoffs, many fans _____ (root) for us.

were waiting **9.** Manuel and I _____ (wait) for the bus when we heard the news.

am holding **10.** I _____ (hold) my breath as I wait to hear the news about the playoffs.

Next Step Write three sentences. Use the present continuous tense in one, the past continuous tense in another, and the future continuous tense in the third. Then mix up the order and read your sentences to a partner. Have him or her tell which tense you have used in each sentence.

© Houghton Mifflin Harcourt Publishing Company

Irregular Verbs

Most verbs in the English language are said to be **regular** because they follow a simple, predictable pattern—when a regular verb goes into the past, you just add *ed* to it. The rest of the verbs in the English language are called **irregular.** They do not follow this simple pattern. For most irregular verbs, the whole word changes in the past tense. When an irregular verb is used with *has, had,* and *have* (as a past participle), the base verb changes again. (See pages 481 and 722 in *Write Source* for a list of common irregular verbs.)

Examples

	Present Tense	Past Tense	Past Participle
Regular	I talk.	I talked.	I **have** talked.
Irregular	I speak.	I spoke.	I **have** spoken.

 **Directions** Fill in the past tense and past participle of these verbs. They are all irregular.

Present Tense	Past Tense	Past Participle
1. I am happy.	I _was_ happy.	I have _been_ happy.
2. He bites his lip.	He _bit_ his lip.	He has _bitten_ his lip.
3. She breaks dishes.	She _broke_ dishes.	She has _broken_ dishes.
4. I catch a cold.	I _caught_ a cold.	I have _caught_ a cold.
5. She does yoga.	She _did_ yoga.	She has _done_ yoga.
6. I drink milk.	I _drank_ milk.	I have _drunk_ milk.
7. He eats pizza.	He _ate_ pizza.	He has _eaten_ pizza.
8. I fall down.	I _fell_ down.	I had _fallen_ down.
9. She flies a plane.	She _flew_ a plane.	She has _flown_ a plane.
10. I give blood.	I _gave_ blood.	I have _given_ blood.

© Houghton Mifflin Harcourt Publishing Company

Present Tense	Past Tense	Past Participle
11. They go to town.	They _went_ to town.	They have _gone_ to town.
12. We hide from Joe.	We _hid_ from Joe.	We have _hidden_ from Joe.
13. I know the answer.	I _knew_ the answer.	I had _known_ the answer.
14. She leads the band.	She _led_ the band.	She has _led_ the band.
15. They ride bikes.	They _rode_ bikes.	They have _ridden_ bikes.
16. I run fast.	I _ran_ fast.	I had _ran_ (run) fast.
17. They see me.	They _saw_ me.	They have _seen_ me.
18. We sing songs.	We _sang_ songs.	We have _sung_ songs.
19. I swim swiftly.	I _swam_ swiftly.	I have _swam_ (swum) swiftly.
20. I take chances.	I _took_ chances.	I have _taken_ chances.
21. He throws fits.	He _threw_ fits.	He has _thrown_ fits.
22. We wear hats.	We _wore_ hats.	We have _worn_ hats.
23. I build models.	I _built_ models.	I have _built_ models.
24. We ring the bell.	We _rang_ the bell.	We have _rung_ the bell.
25. They grow apples.	They _grew_ apples.	They have _grown_ apples.

Next Step Find a paragraph (or two) in a book or magazine. Look at all the verbs and see if you can identify them as regular or irregular.

© Houghton Mifflin Harcourt Publishing Company

Transitive and Intransitive Verbs

Transitive verbs "transfer" their action to a direct object (and sometimes to an indirect object). The direct object completes the meaning of the sentence, as in the examples that follow. An **intransitive** verb completes its meaning without an object. (See 728.2–728.3 and 730.1 in *Write Source* for more information.)

Examples

Transitive Verb:

Some explorers gave kings and queens gold.

- *Direct Object:* A direct object receives the direct action of the verb. It answers the question *who?* or *what?* after the verb. Some explorers "gave" what? ("gold")

- *Indirect Object:* An indirect object receives the action of the verb indirectly. It tells *to whom* or *for whom* something is done. Some explorers gave "gold" to whom? ("kings and queens")

Intransitive Verb:

Some explorers gave up.

- *No Object:* An intransitive verb does not transfer its action. Its action is complete without an object.

Intransitive Verb:

Some explorers gave up before finding gold.

- *Object of a Preposition:* If an object ("gold") follows a preposition ("before"), it is an object of the preposition; it is not an object of the verb.

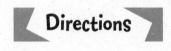 **Directions** Write "T" in front of sentences with transitive verbs and "I" in front of sentences with intransitive verbs. For each transitive verb, underline the direct object and circle any indirect objects. The first one has been done for you.

_____*T*_____ **1.** Early Egyptians sailed their <u>boats</u> only on the Nile River.

_____ **2.** Ancient Egyptians thought of the world as a flat rectangle with four

pillars holding up the sky.

© Houghton Mifflin Harcourt Publishing Company

_____ **3.** Egyptian merchants imported ebony and ivory.

_____ **4.** Other early explorers, such as the Phoenicians, journeyed through the Mediterranean Sea into the Atlantic Ocean to Britain.

_____ **5.** Phoenicians sold other explorers valuables and food.

_____ **6.** But rather than buy or trade, many explorers attacked ships and took their valuable cargo.

_____ **7.** The Vikings stole gold, silver, and jewelry from many settlements.

_____ **8.** Around the year 1000, Leif Ericson and his band of Vikings stayed in North America at Newfoundland for the winter.

_____ **9.** Then in 1492, in search of the East Indies Islands, Christopher Columbus discovered the West Indies and Cuba.

_____ **10.** On the return trip, Columbus gave his officers hammocks, an idea he got from the islanders.

_____ **11.** Columbus never told his sailors the distance they had gone because the crew was afraid of sailing off the edge of the world.

_____ **12.** Amerigo Vespucci, the first to discover that America was a new continent, supplied other sailors maps of the New World.

Next Step Some verbs, such as *drive, read,* and *play,* can be either transitive or intransitive. Choose one of those verbs and write a sentence using it as a transitive verb, and then write another sentence using it as an intransitive verb. Afterward, see if you can think of at least 10 more verbs that can be both transitive and intransitive.

© Houghton Mifflin Harcourt Publishing Company

Identifying Verbals

Hidden in many pieces of writing are secret agents known as **verbals.** A verbal is a verb acting as another part of speech; it's a verb in disguise. **Gerunds, participles,** and **infinitives** are verbals. (For more information, see page 485 and 730.2–730.4 in *Write Source.*)

Examples

A *gerund* is a verb form ending in *ing* that is used as a noun.

Shopping **is excellent recreation.**

(The noun "shopping" is the subject of this sentence.)

A *participle* is a verb form ending in *ed* or *ing* that is used as an adjective.

The <u>butterfly</u> fluttering **near the daisy** <u>is</u> **a monarch.**

(The adjective "fluttering" modifies "butterfly.")

An *infinitive* is a verb form introduced by the word "to" that can be used as a noun, an adjective, or an adverb.

I <u>plan</u> to read **a book on Saturday.**

(The infinitive "to read" is a noun used as a direct object.)

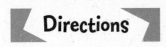 **Directions** In the following paragraph, verbals are underlined. Above each of these words, identify what kind of verbal it is—gerund, participle, or infinitive. The first one has been done for you.

participle
1 Idalia, <u>bored</u> with the usual presents, asked for a pet for her birthday.

2 <u>Walking</u> a dog of her own had been her dream for a long time. A poodle puppy

3 <u>wagging</u> its tail in a pet store caught her eye. <u>Hoping</u> for this pet, Idalia went

4 to the store every day <u>to look</u> at the beloved pup. On her birthday, Idalia and

5 her mom hurried to the store <u>to buy</u> the poodle. Idalia named the <u>excited</u>

6 puppy Inglebert, which means "unusually intelligent." <u>Playing</u> fetch and

7 <u>teaching</u> Inglebert new tricks now take up much of Idalia's time.

© Houghton Mifflin Harcourt Publishing Company

Directions In the following passage, underline the verbals. Above each of these words, identify what kind of verbal it is—gerund, participle, or infinitive. The first one has been done for you.

participle

1 <u>Pausing</u> to shake the water off her fur, the Labrador retriever

2 scrambled up the beach and dropped the tennis ball at her master's feet.

3 Sighing, he picked it up to throw again. It splashed far out in the lake.

4 Retrieving the yellow object was all that mattered to the dog.

5 Determined to continue the game, she bounded into the water and paddled

6 to the ball. Grabbing it in her mouth and turning toward shore, she swam

7 back as if she were in a race. Soaked but happy, she climbed out of the

8 water, shook again, dropped the ball, and backed expectantly for the

9 next throw.

10 He wondered how many times it would take before the dog would be

11 too tired to swim after the ball. Feeling the warm sun on his shoulders,

12 he decided that this was a good day to test her stamina. "I've got all

13 afternoon," he mused, "and throwing the ball is the easy part. Let's just

14 see how long it takes for her to lose her enthusiasm."

Next Step On your own paper, write a paragraph about an animal. Use at least one example of each kind of verbal. Then exchange paragraphs with a classmate and circle and label the verbals in each other's work.

© Houghton Mifflin Harcourt Publishing Company

Using Specific Verbs

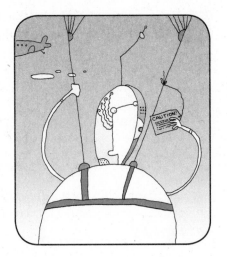

A sentence like "The plane flew past Ralphy" is too general to create a vivid image or word picture. A reader can't see how the plane was flying, or how close it flew to Ralphy, or what it sounded like.

On the other hand, if the sentence were to say "The plane screamed past Ralphy," the reader would be able to see things more clearly. A specific verb like *scream* makes the sentence come alive for the reader. Specific verbs add punch to writing. (See "Action Verbs" on page 480 in *Write Source*.)

Directions | In each of the sentences below, substitute one vivid verb for the verb and adverb in parentheses. The first one has been done for you.

1. Brett _____*tore*_____ *(quickly went)* across the burning sand.

2. Donna _____ *(carefully read)* the tag on her parachute.

3. Kevin _____ *(went quickly)* past the sleeping Doberman.

4. Suzy _____ *(moved quickly)* past the other runners.

5. Miss Tinely _____ *(spoke loudly)* at her daydreaming friend.

6. Tim _____ *(looked quickly)* at the fuel gauge.

7. The white rhinoceros _____ *(walked heavily)* down the ramp.

8. The mice _____ *(moved in all directions)* to their holes.

9. The writer _____ *(looked blankly)* at the unopened letter.

10. The boys _____ *(talked negatively)* about the football game for half an hour.

11. Shavonne _____ *(drank noisily)* her milkshake.

12. Jesse _____ *(ate slowly)* his hamburger.

© Houghton Mifflin Harcourt Publishing Company

Directions In the paragraph below, substitute a vivid verb for each verb in parentheses.

1   I always thought it was impossible to go sledding without snow.

2   But that was before I tried "ice blocking." Some friends and I

3   *(got)* _____ six 10-pound blocks of ice from a local gas

4   station. Then we *(went)* _____ to a nearby park and

5   *(took)* _____ the heavy blocks to the top of a large

6   grassy hill. I *(saw)* _____ my friends as they

7   *(moved)* _____ down the steep slope; they

8   *(sat)* _____ carefully on towels laid on top of the blocks

9   so they wouldn't *(fall)* _____ off. Finally I

10   *(got)* _____ the courage to try. Down the hill I

11   *(moved)* _____ . I hadn't realized that an ice block

12   could *(go)* _____ so fast. Then, near the bottom, I

13   *(hit)* _____ a bump and *(fell)* _____

14   off, rolling over and over in the grass and mud. Before long, I was

15   *(covered)* _____ with dirt and grime. I

16   *(liked)* _____ "ice blocking," but sledding on snow is

17   definitely much cleaner.

Next Step Circle five of the vivid verbs you used above. Now look up each one in a thesaurus and choose a new verb to write next to the circled one. In each one, which verb do you like best, the circled verb or the one from the thesaurus? Why?

© Houghton Mifflin Harcourt Publishing Company

Adjectives

Let's say you are writing about someone whose pen suddenly popped apart during an essay test. Adjectives could help you make this action seem real for a reader. Colorful adjectives add life to writing and help you tell an effective story. However, don't overuse them; otherwise your writing will sound forced or unnatural. (For more information about choosing effective modifiers, see pages 486–489 and 732.1–732.3 in *Write Source*.)

Example

After the top half of Jorge's pen rocketed across the room, the ink cartridge and metal spring followed in its path. He was left with the useless bottom half.

(The colored words are all adjectives. They help a reader visualize exactly what has happened.)

 **Directions** Beneath each of the frequently used adjectives below, list at least four colorful and creative synonyms. (Don't know what a synonym is? Look it up in *Write Source*.)

nice

1. _____
2. _____
3. _____
4. _____

bad

1. _____
2. _____
3. _____
4. _____

great

1. _____
2. _____
3. _____
4. _____

old

1. _____
2. _____
3. _____
4. _____

© Houghton Mifflin Harcourt Publishing Company

 **Directions**

Read and enjoy the following description of a brave, determined artist. Circle at least 20 colorful adjectives, in addition to the one already circled, in this true story.

The Blind Seer

1　Our family's longtime friend Armand Merizon is more than an artist. He

2　is a rebel, a man of vision, and something of a prophet.

3　When I was 13, supposedly asleep in my upstairs bedroom, his (oversized)

4　personality would fill our house. He and my parents would debate for hours

5　about politics, religion, art, and the state of the environment. His roar and

6　his chuckle were so deep they seemed to knock the pictures crooked on the

7　walls. In my mind, I could picture his green army coat with its bottomless

8　pockets, his full, black beard and his waving hands. The blue-gray smoke from

9　his Jamaican cigar would cloud up through the furnace vents, prick my nos-

10　trils, fill my lungs, and cling to my pajamas. I could not have known then how

11　much of him I would take into my life.

12　Today he is nearly seventy and gradually going blind. Fifty years of

13　experimentation with light and design and texture of paint on canvas are

14　being forced to an early end. He has always filled the center of his canvases

15　with a sparkling, brilliant light. That bright center shows the intense moment

16　in which he sees and feels beauty. And now it is exactly the center of his

17　vision, the bull's-eye, that he cannot see. Yet he has told me he will not stop

18　painting until his nose touches the canvas.

19　He used to paint landscapes and seascapes in fine detail. He can't see

20　the details anymore. But now he paints with fierce joy—free forms in colors

21　that make rainbows look pale. Now you can feel his anger and hear his

22　laughter in his abstract designs. He has always rejected the ordinary. But

23　now, with his beard turned to gray, he loves life more than ever. And he sees

24　it in excellent detail with his inward eye.

© Houghton Mifflin Harcourt Publishing Company

Special Adjectives

There are times when you will use special adjectives in your writing. Some of these adjectives are demonstrative adjectives, compound adjectives, indefinite adjectives, and predicate adjectives. (See 732.4, 732.5, 734.1, and 734.2 in *Write Source* for more information.)

Examples

Demonstrative Adjectives:

This oak tree is taller than that pine tree.
A demonstrative adjective helps point out a noun. "This" and "these" point out a nearby noun. "That" and "those" point out a more distant noun. (When "this," "that," "these," and "those" follow nouns, they are considered pronouns and not adjectives.)

Compound Adjectives:

A shortleaf pine tree has yellow-green needles and scale-like bark.
A compound adjective is made up of two or more words and is often hyphenated.

Indefinite Adjectives:

Most parks have some trees.
An indefinite adjective gives an approximate number or quantity.

Predicate Adjectives:

The trees are old and gnarled.
A predicate adjective follows a linking verb and describes the subject.

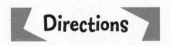 **Directions** — Write a "C" above each compound adjective, a "D" above each demonstrative adjective, an "I" above each indefinite adjective, and a "P" above each predicate adjective. The first sentence has been done for you.

1   Many *[I]* different trees grow in North America, and wherever you live,

2   you can see some *[I]* trees. More than 600 different species of trees range

3   across these United States. Most species are native to this continent, but a

4   few species were brought over from several faraway places. Many trees,

5   such as the common juniper, have widespread habitats, and some species,

6   like the fox-tail pine, are found in just a few remote areas.

© Houghton Mifflin Harcourt Publishing Company

7   To be a tree, a plant must be tall (at least 15 feet tall) and have

8   well-developed branches and a single woody stem. Trees have two types of

9   leaves. Cone-bearing evergreen trees have leaves (or needles) that stay on

10 the branches, while other trees have deciduous leaves that fall off each year.

11 These deciduous trees include oaks, maples, and elms. Although few people

12 would believe it, even cacti can be trees. The tree-sized saguaro is found in

13 the Southwest, produces fruit, and has funnel-shaped flowers that have a

14 melonlike smell. The trees that may be the most easily recognized are in

15 the redwood family. This family includes those mighty giants, the redwood

16 and sequoia. Many sequoias reach 12 feet in diameter and grow over 250

17 feet tall. These reddish-brown giants are more than 3,000 years old.

18 Redwoods are thinner and taller than sequoias. Some have grown more

19 than 350 feet tall. Those giant redwoods have a swampland cousin in

20 Florida called the bald cypress. These oversized trees have scalelike bark,

21 yellow-green needles, and round cones. A bald cypress grows to be 125 feet

22 tall and to have a 5-foot-diameter base.

Next Step Write a list of 10 descriptive adjectives. Then see how many compound adjectives you can create by adding another word to each adjective.

© Houghton Mifflin Harcourt Publishing Company

Using Adjectives to Compare

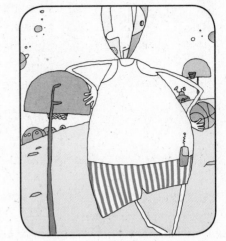

Special forms of adjectives are used to compare nouns. (See page 487 and 734.4–734.6 in *Write Source* for more information and examples.)

Examples

Comparative Form:

I am taller than my brother.

(To compare two persons, places, things or ideas.)

Superlative Form:

I am the tallest basketball player on the team.

(To compare three or more persons, places, things or ideas.)

One-syllable, and some two-syllable, adjectives form comparatives and superlatives using *er* and *est* endings:

big, bigger, biggest

Most adjectives with two or more syllables form the comparative and superlative by pairing the words *more* and *most* (*less, least*) with the positive form:

terrible, more terrible, most terrible

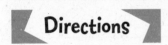 **Directions** Fill in the following blanks with the comparative and superlative forms of the adjectives given.

	Positive	Comparative	Superlative
1.	*great*		
2.	*smart*		
3.	*caring*		
4.	*terrific*		
5.	*radiant*		
6.	*weird*		

© Houghton Mifflin Harcourt Publishing Company

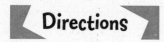 **Directions** Now imagine that you are a movie reviewer, and in a short paragraph, review your favorite—or least favorite—movie. Try to use a number of the adjectives (in one form or another) from the list on the previous page.

Movie Review Paragraph

_____

_____

_____

_____

_____

_____

_____

_____

_____

_____

_____

_____

_____

_____

Next Step Exchange paragraphs with a classmate. Read each other's review. Then circle any comparative or superlative forms used.

© Houghton Mifflin Harcourt Publishing Company

Adverbs 1

As part of a unit on aeronautics, one student is testing his paper airplane design for the rest of the class. If you were to describe this scene, how could using adverbs help to make the action seem more real? By adding spice and detail to the verbs and by bringing the action into focus—that's how. See the example below. (Also, see pages 490 and 736 in *Write Source* for more about adverbs.)

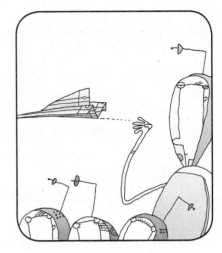

Example

As Bryan expertly snapped his wrist, his sleek airplane sailed smoothly and surely above the heads of his classmates.

("Expertly," "smoothly," and "surely" are all one-word adverbs.)

 **Directions** In the following sentences, locate and underline all of the one-word adverbs. The number of adverbs in each sentence is given in parentheses. The first one has been done for you. (*Note:* Do not include prepositional phrases used as adverbs.)

1. The pilot announced, "Thunderstorms are <u>quickly</u> building to our left." *(1)*

2. John's mother hardly dared to look. *(1)*

3. Someone quietly said that she saw sparks suddenly flicker from one engine. *(2)*

4. John, a seven-year-old boy, excitedly looked around. *(2)*

5. Soon it was time to land in New York. *(1)*

6. Travelers filed quickly off the plane and hurriedly scattered everywhere. *(3)*

7. John and his mother searched the crowd anxiously for his aunt. *(1)*

8. Suddenly the airport was without any light. *(1)*

9. Now to move anywhere was very difficult. *(3)*

10. Thanks to emergency lights, passengers somehow found the baggage-claim area in the dark. *(1)*

© Houghton Mifflin Harcourt Publishing Company

Adverbs 2

Adverbs, like adjectives, have three forms: *positive*, *comparative*, and *superlative*. And like adjectives, the spelling of comparative and superlative adverbs depends on the number of syllables in the positive form. (See pages 490–491 and 738.3–738.4 in *Write Source* for more examples.)

Examples

	One Syllable	Two or More Syllables
Positive:	**fast**	**quickly**
Comparative:	**faster**	**more quickly**
Superlative:	**fastest**	**most quickly**

 **Directions** Use each of the following adverbs in a sentence. Use the adverb in the form indicated in parentheses. The first one has been done for you.

1. firmly *(comparative)* _Mom gives orders more firmly than Dad._

2. slow *(superlative)* _____

_____

3. strangely *(positive)* _____

_____

4. frequently *(comparative)* _____

_____

5. rarely *(positive)* _____

_____

6. loudly *(superlative)* _____

_____

Next Step Share your results with a classmate. Discuss any of your partner's sentences in which the adverbs are incorrectly formed.

© Houghton Mifflin Harcourt Publishing Company

Types of Adverbs

There are four basic types of adverbs: *time*, *place*, *manner*, and *degree*. (See pages 490 and 736 in *Write Source* for more about adverbs.)

Examples

Time:

Terri never misses gymnastics.
Adverbs of time tell "when," "how often," and "how long."

Place:

She does flips outside in the summer.
Adverbs of place tell "where," "to where," or "from where."

Manner:

She warms up gradually.
Adverbs of manner often end in "ly" and tell "how" something is done.

Degree:

She practices her routine entirely before a meet.
Adverbs of degree tell "how much" or "how little."

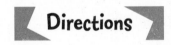 **Directions** — In the sentences below, underline the adverbs. In front of each sentence, write "T" for time, "P" for place, "M" for manner, or "D" for degree. The first one has been done for you.

___M___ **1.** Angel moved <u>quickly</u> through the lunch line.

_____ **2.** Please step outside and clean the erasers.

_____ **3.** The seventh graders often play softball at noon.

_____ **4.** There is scarcely enough paper for the project.

_____ **5.** At the spring concert, the eighth graders sang beautifully.

_____ **6.** Tara easily won the swimming race.

_____ **7.** The eighth graders are going on a field trip tomorrow.

_____ **8.** Because of the rain, we won't go outside for recess.

© Houghton Mifflin Harcourt Publishing Company

Prepositions

A **preposition** is a word that introduces a prepositional phrase. *"In the air," "over the hills," "on the ground"* are all prepositional phrases introduced by prepositions. (See pages 494, 495, and 742 in your *Write Source*.)

Example

The boy in the aviator suit **wanted to fly.**
("In the aviator suit" is a prepositional phrase starting with the preposition "in." The phrase is used as an adjective to describe the boy. "To fly" is an infinitive—a verb with the word "to" in front of it. It is used as the direct object in the sentence.)

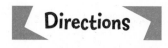 **Directions** Underline the prepositional phrases in the following passage. (Remember prepositional phrases are used as adjectives or adverbs.) Be careful not to confuse prepositional phrases with infinitive phrases.

1   Have you ever dreamed of flying—by yourself, without a plane? Well,

2 at some time in the future, it may be more than a dream. Some day you may

3 wake up in the morning, strap on your power pack, and fly away. Imagine

4 jetting to school in the morning or to the park in the afternoon. Think

5 of the time you would save, not to mention the view.

6   But, there are still some minor problems with the power-pack idea.

7 Imagine what it would be like with thousands of people flying in all directions

8 at the same time. Then there's the weather. How do you handle storms

9 in the summer or blizzards in the winter when all you have for protection is an

10 aviator suit? And what happens if you run short of fuel while flying?

11   Maybe solo flight isn't such a good idea. Now that I think about it,

12 what's wrong with planes, trains, and automobiles?

© Houghton Mifflin Harcourt Publishing Company

Coordinating Conjunctions

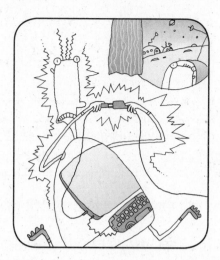

Parallel structures (two or more ideas worded in the same way) are pleasing to our "reading ear." They focus attention on certain words, add rhythm and music to sentences, and create powerful ideas.

Words, phrases, and ideas that are parallel are often connected by **coordinating conjunctions** (*and, but, so, for,* and *yet*). To make ideas parallel in your own writing, make sure that the ideas are equal and are worded in the same way. (See page 496 and 744.1 in *Write Source* for more information.)

Examples

I hear, and I forget. I see, and I remember. I do, and I understand.

— **Chinese proverb**

(The coordinating conjunction "and" links three pairs of independent clauses.)

The book to read is not the one that thinks for you, but the one that makes you think.

— **James McCosh**

(The coordinating conjunction "but" links two independent clauses that are worded in the same way.)

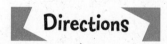 **Directions** Complete each of the following sentences by adding a word, a phrase, or a clause that is parallel to the underlined portion of the sentence.

1. Summer can be a leisurely time for <u>reading a good book</u> or _____

    _____ .

2. When my friends and I get together for a movie marathon, we usually rent at

    least <u>one action movie,</u> _____ ,

    and _____ .

3. <u>Packing my suitcase for our vacation</u> is as much fun for me as _____

    _____ .

© Houghton Mifflin Harcourt Publishing Company

4. So we don't get bored on family trips, we always take along these

things: <u>paper and pencils,</u> _____ , and __

_____ .

5. Labor Day signals <u>the end of summer vacation</u> and _____

_____ .

6. One day we drove all morning and saw nothing but cactus and sagebrush; then

we drove all afternoon and _____ .

Example

Incorrect Sentence:
A vegetarian's diet consists of grains, plants, and <u>the products of plants</u>.

Correct Sentence:
A vegetarian's diet consists of grains, plants, and <u>plant products</u>.

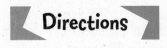 **Directions** Underline the idea that upsets the parallel structure in each of the following sentences. Then, on your own paper rewrite the sentence so that all the ideas are parallel.

1. Today there are millions of vegetarians in the United States, and Europe

has millions of them, too.

2. Pythagorus, a very famous vegetarian, traveled throughout ancient Greece

in search of truth, knowledge, and what life means.

3. Another famous vegetarian, Sir Thomas More, was tried for high treason

and then they found him guilty.

4. Vegetarians can now get special dishes at restaurants, in hospitals, and

vegetarian dishes are also available on airplanes.

© Houghton Mifflin Harcourt Publishing Company

Correlative Conjunctions

Conjunctions join words or groups of words. **Correlative conjunctions** are used in pairs. (For more information about correlative conjunctions, see page 496 and 744.2 in *Write Source*.)

Correlative Conjunctions:
either, or
neither, nor
not only, but also
both, and
whether, or

Example

Both bicycling and ice-skating equipment have changed over the past 100 years.

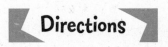
Directions From the list above, use a pair of correlative conjunctions to complete each sentence below. (Choose the pair of conjunctions that makes the most sense.)

1. _____ baseball _____ football has been around

   since the 1870s.

2. _____ Abner Doubleday _____ someone else

   "invented" modern baseball is still being debated.

3. Before 1875, baseball catchers had _____ gloves

   _____ masks to protect themselves from a pitched ball; they

   stopped the ball with their chests.

4. In the first football games, players could _____ pick up the

   round football _____ run with it.

© Houghton Mifflin Harcourt Publishing Company

5. Girls were not supposed to fish or row a boat, but they could try

_____ archery _____ croquet.

6. People enjoyed swimming _____ it was in a pool

_____ at the beach.

7. Whatever name it was known by, _____ badminton

_____ poona, this sport became popular among wealthy

people in the 1870s.

8. Polo was introduced from India, and it was played _____

outside _____ indoors.

9. _____ sledding _____ ice-skating were popular

winter sports.

10. Ice skates were made with _____ wooden

_____ iron blades and had to be sharpened often.

11. Hockey requires _____ strong skating skills, _____

strong stick skills.

12. _____ football _____ wrestling is strictly for

boys anymore.

Next Step Write five sentences about a sport you enjoy. Use all five sets of correlative
conjunctions listed on page 179. Read your sentences to a classmate.

© Houghton Mifflin Harcourt Publishing Company

Subordinating Conjunctions

A subordinating conjunction connects a dependent clause to an independent clause. (See pages 496, 498, and 746.1 in *Write Source* for more information about subordinating conjunctions.)

Example

Subordinating Conjunction and Clause:
Fran made the team <u>because</u> **of her powerful serves**.

 Add a dependent clause to the independent clause using the connecting subordinating conjunction that is given. The first sentence has been done for you.

1. The modern Olympic games began in 1896 <u>because</u>   *a French educator*

   thought they could make the world more peaceful. _____ .

2. A sport often becomes more popular <u>after</u> _____

   _____ .

3. Some people think bowling should be an Olympic sport <u>although</u> _____

   _____ .

4. An Olympic gymnast makes every move look graceful <u>as if</u> _____

   _____ .

5. Water polo should be an Olympic sport <u>as long as</u> _____

   _____ .

6. Some athletes should finish their education <u>before</u> _____

   _____ .

© Houghton Mifflin Harcourt Publishing Company

7. I could be an Olympic athlete <u>if</u> _____

_____ .

8. The best athletes should compete in the Olympics <u>in order that</u> _____

_____ .

9. I would love to travel to the Olympic games <u>so</u> _____

_____ .

10. I won't be ready for the Olympics <u>until</u> _____

_____ .

11. The Olympics should be held in my city <u>because</u> _____

_____ .

12. I like to swim <u>when</u> _____

_____ .

13. Students should have less homework <u>while</u> _____

_____ .

14. The Olympic games take place in many countries <u>where</u> _____

_____ .

15. The games are televised live <u>unless</u> _____

_____ .

Next Step Write a paragraph telling what it would be like for you to attend or participate in the Olympic games. Include at least two sentences that use subordinating conjunctions.

© Houghton Mifflin Harcourt Publishing Company

Interjections

An **interjection** is a word or phrase used to express strong emotion or surprise. *Wow!* and *Yikes!* are two examples. A comma or an exclamation point is usually used to separate an interjection from the rest of the sentence. (See page 746 in *Write Source*.)

> **Directions** Underline each interjection in the sentences that follow.

1. "Good grief, Mr. Yates, we had a test on fractions yesterday," said Al.

2. "Hallelujah!" yelled our teacher. "A test a day is good for the soul."

3. "Yeah!" blurted Clarisse. "But what about our minds?"

4. "SHSHSHSHSHSH!" hissed Mr. Yates.

5. "Holy fractions, Mr. Yates. If we were happy every time you gave a test, we'd be the weirdest eighth graders on earth," Clarisse explained.

6. "Hey, Clarisse, stop the wisecracks," replied Mr. Yates patiently.

7. "Wow, Mr. Yates," answered Clarisse, "I was just being honest."

8. "I know," explained Mr. Yates. "But, for goodness sake, you didn't think I was being serious, did you?"

9. "Whew! That's what I was hoping!" exclaimed Clarisse.

10. "Okay, let's get back to the test."

© Houghton Mifflin Harcourt Publishing Company

| yes | great | oh no | stop | all right |
| hooray | wow | whew | duck | watch out |

Directions — Use the words from the above list to complete the sentences below. Be sure to use capital letters when necessary.

1. " _____Hooray_____ for our team! We just won the championship," yelled Dave.

2. "Did you see that last pass? _____, it doesn't get any better," said George.

3. Sheila screamed, "_____!"

4. "_____," cried Sean. "There's a penalty flag on the field."

5. "_____," moaned Dustin, "that probably means the touchdown won't count."

6. Then Dave cheered saying, "_____! The penalty was on the other team. See the referee's signal? Now we can celebrate."

7. As the group started for the field, a security officer yelled, "_____! No one is allowed on the field."

8. A happy player threw a football toward the crowd, so Sheila said, "_____!"

9. "_____!" the guard said. "A bus is coming through."

10. "_____! That was a close call. Thanks for warning us," Dustin exclaimed.

Next Step Team up with a classmate and create a brief scene in which two or more characters express strong emotion or surprise. Consider performing this scene for your classmates.

© Houghton Mifflin Harcourt Publishing Company

Parts of Speech Review

When you write, some words can be used in many different ways. For example, a word may be a noun in one sentence and an adjective in the next sentence. Knowing the eight parts of speech will help you to understand how a word can be used in a sentence. (See the sample sentences below in which the word *dog* is used as four different parts of speech. Turn to page 748 in *Write Source* for more information.)

Examples

      noun   adjective

The dog barked to get some more dog food.

                  verb   adverb

The runner was dogging it because he was dog tired.

Directions   Label the part of speech for each underlined word in this excerpt from a speech by George Graham Vest. He was a United States senator from Missouri from 1879 to 1903. He made this speech while he was a lawyer representing a man whose dog was killed. Vest's speech helped him win the case.

nouns ☐ ☐ ☐ ☐	**adverbs** ☐ ☐ ☐ ☐	**conjunctions** ☐ ☐ ☐ ☐
verbs ☐ ☐ ☐ ☐	**adjectives** ☐ ☐ ☐ ☐	**interjections** ☐ ☐
pronouns ☐ ☐ ☐ ☐	**prepositions** ☐ ☐ ☐ ☐	

1   The best friend a man has in the world may turn <u>against</u> him and

2   become his enemy. His son or daughter <u>whom</u> he has reared with loving <u>care</u>

3   <u>may</u> prove ungrateful. The money that a man has, <u>he</u> may lose. It flies

4   away from him, perhaps <u>when</u> he needs it most. A man's reputation may be

5   <u>sacrificed</u> in a moment of <u>ill-considered</u> action. The one <u>absolutely</u>

6   unselfish friend that a man can have in this <u>selfish</u> world, the one that

7   <u>never</u> deserts him, the <u>one</u> that never proves ungrateful <u>or</u> treacherous is

8   his dog. <u>Yes</u>, a man's dog <u>stands</u> by him in prosperity and in <u>poverty</u>, in

© Houghton Mifflin Harcourt Publishing Company

9   health and in sickness. He will sleep <u>on</u> the cold ground, where the <u>wintry</u>

10   winds blow and the snow drives <u>fiercely</u>, if only he may be <u>near</u> his master's

11   side. When all other friends desert, he remains. <u>Oh</u>, when riches take

12   wings, and <u>reputation</u> falls to pieces, he is as constant in his love as the sun

13   in <u>its</u> journey <u>through</u> the heavens. <u>And</u> when the last scene of all comes,

14   and death takes his master, no matter if all other <u>friends</u> pursue their way,

15   <u>there</u> by the graveside will the noble dog <u>be</u> found, his head between his

16   paws, his eyes sad, <u>but</u> open in alert watchfulness, <u>faithful</u> and true even in

17   death.

Directions Pick one of the following words and use it in several sentences as at least three different parts of speech. Then pick another word and try again.

ape   back   run   green   hand   light   like   out   small   stop

_____

_____

_____

_____

_____

_____

Next Step Wow, write a sentence and happily use all eight parts of speech in it (just like this one). Then work together with a classmate and write three sentences that include all eight parts of speech in each sentence. See if you can write one using 10 or fewer words!

© Houghton Mifflin Harcourt Publishing Company